The Home Cook's Guide to JOURNALING

The Home Cook's Guide to JOURNALING

Paige Rhodes

LARK
New York

New York

An Imprint of Sterling Publishing Co., Inc.
1166 Avenue of the Americas
New York, NY 10036

ISBN 978-1-4547-1081-3

Distributed in Canada by Sterling Publishing Co., Inc.
c/o Canadian Manda Group, 664 Annette Street
Toronto, Ontario M6S 2C8, Canada

For information about custom editions, special sales,
and premium and corporate purchases, please contact Sterling Special Sales
at 800-805-5489 or specialsales@sterlingpublishing.com.

Manufactured in China

2 4 6 8 10 9 7 5 3 1

sterlingpublishing.com
larkcrafts.com

Written and photographed by Paige Rhodes
Cover design by Valerie Hou
Interior design by Leah Germann

Additional picture credits—see page 160

CONTENTS

INTRODUCTION

Planning and organization have always been a huge part of who I am. Even as a child, I took pride in marking items off my to-do list and taking care of my notebook. My lists may look a lot different these days, but the thrill of completing tasks and planning my week is still a major source of satisfaction for me. I've dabbled in every type of planner, bought pricey personalized notebooks, and attempted going digital, but nothing stuck as *the* perfect method for structuring my life. That is, until I started using a blank journal and customized it to my needs. When used properly, a simple notebook brings clarity and order to the chaos of your everyday life.

After years of using premade planners with little success, I realized that I was mostly filling them with recipes and grocery lists, while leaving other sections empty. Although I may be a food blogger by trade, it dawned on me that meal planning is a major source of stress for many people,

no matter their cooking skills. I can't tell you how many times I've heard someone say that they often don't cook because they don't have time to plan ahead. For those of you who are like me and value saving money on groceries, helping the environment, and creating delicious and nutritious meals, then journaling will transform your life.

You're probably wondering just how this book is going to put you on the path to weeknight supper success. As you read it, you'll receive valuable advice on how to grocery shop; what tools, spices, and condiments to keep on hand; and how to use the ingredients you already have to whip up a tasty meal. You'll discover over fifty simple recipes that will soon become staples for everyday meals and special dinners. You'll also find all the information you need to build your journal the way that works best for you, along with templates that you can use to get started.

PART 1

COOKING
THAT
JOINS THE
DOTS!

"If you want to change the world, pick up your pen and write."

–Martin Luther

1

THE
JOURNALING
CONNECTION

Considering we're in the age of smartphones, keeping a pen-and-paper journal might seem like an archaic way to plan meals and make grocery lists. But going offline and using a simple hard-copy format frees you from distractions. Online, one second you're making a grocery list, the next you're checking social media or replying to a notification that popped up on your screen. Journaling is a great way to focus as you plan your meals, list your grocery essentials, and budget for the week ahead.

It's Time to Try Journaling

This book will show you how to take a blank journal and turn it into your very own recipe- and meal-planning hub. Gone will be the days of fumbling through your purse or pocket to find that elusive sticky note with the day's grocery list. With my help, you can cook delicious meals at home and save time and money.

Journaling is the key to the new organized you. It's more than just keeping a diary, jotting to-do lists down on sticky notes, or budgeting on the back of an envelope. Journaling is a systematic way to organize the things you need to do and set priorities using lists and page layouts you draw yourself. This type of journaling uses a personalized notebook that helps you arrange your life and make it more organized and efficient. Many people use their journal to make their day-to-day tasks quicker and easier to complete. A journal also makes sure all your lists and meal plans are stored safely in one place.

The key to keeping a journal is to find a system that works for you. Some journalers love setting up elaborate pages and filling them in with colored pens and fancy hand-lettering. Others favor a no-frills look.

SYMBOLS

Most journalers use a system of symbols to help them identify different types of tasks and the status of each one. Here are examples you can use.

- ■ the task
- ✔ task completed
- / task no longer necessary
- → task carried over to another list

FIRST STEPS

At its simplest, all you need is a notebook and pen to start journaling. Building your journal pages is the fun part of customizing your own notebook. Here's a quick guide to how to start.

- Begin by adding page numbers to your notebook. Leave about five pages at the front blank, then start numbering from there. You can number the pages all at the same time, or do it as you go.

- Use the blank pages at the front to create a list of pages you want to refer to again, perhaps because they contain a favorite recipe, a record of your pantry essentials, or plans for a birthday meal. These lists form a table of contents and mean that you'll be able to turn to a recipe you love, a meal plan, or a helpful tip at a moment's notice.

- Weekly meal plans and shopping lists form the core of my journal, but I find monthly and even yearly meal plans useful, particularly for organizing a special birthday celebration or a family get-together for Thanksgiving. Think about which of these plans you're likely to need and add them to your journal, allowing two pages for each layout.

- You can also create pages for anything you'd like to keep track of, including recipes you want to try, healthy eating goals, foodie travel dreams, budgets, and wish lists for kitchen equipment. I recommend leaving two or more pages for each subject.

- There is no "right" way to organize your journal, so include the pages in an order that works for you.

- Get inspiration from journaling blogs and social media accounts, then use any ideas that strike a chord in your own journal. For example, you may find that you like a horizontal Monday through Friday layout, rather than the vertical one on page 140.

- Experiment with colored pens, sticky notes, drawings, doodles, and photos to make your journal your own.

Stress Less

Many people find the act of journaling therapeutic in itself, not to mention the stress it relieves throughout the week. How many times have you wanted to pull your hair out because you're standing in a crowded grocery store trying to figure out what to cook for dinner? Just by being organized and planning your meals, you could save yourself a considerable headache. Plus, you'll save money, especially if you make a budget.

Later in this book, you'll find templates for many of the lists and planners I like to use. These can be helpful if you're intimidated by a blank page and will ensure your journal includes all the layouts you need to get started. For example, there's a pantry template that lists what necessities you need and a budget tracker to make you more aware of how much you're spending at each supermarket trip.

> If there's an item on a list you're worried about forgetting, use a highlighter or different colored pen to make it stand out.

Use the templates on pages 114–153 as inspiration for building your journal pages. You can fill them out, copy them, or use them as the basis for a personalized design.

TRY OUT THESE TEMPLATES
(PAGE 114)

- Yearly and monthly meal planning templates help you map out any important celebrations or holidays.

- Weekly templates come with space for meal planning, shopping lists, and notes about your budget. There is also a separate monthly budget tracker template.

- To keep your kitchen stocked, there's a template for listing the pantry items you'll want to keep on hand. The lists are a suggestion of what you may need—you may not want to use them all, and there will be other things you'll want to add. Look at the lists, then make your own.

- There's also space for listing those big-ticket kitchen items. If you've ever longed for a stand mixer or that fancy Dutch oven, this is where to write that down.

- In addition to these templates, there are also options that allow you to keep track of favorite recipes in books and online, dishes you plan to serve to friends and family, and ideas for breakfasts, lunches, and snacks.

Time Saver

Making those daily trips to the supermarket can eat up a huge chunk of your valuable time. Retrain your brain and, with the help of your journal, do the bulk of your shopping once a week without forgetting items or making impulsive snack buys. The new you will be in and out of the grocery store in a flash.

The key to this time-saving approach is allotting 20 to 30 minutes of your week to making a meal plan and a grocery list in your journal. This could be as simple as sketching a few boxes to check off, or as extravagant as using fancy multicolored hand-lettering to plot your meals. You can copy the templates at the back of this book, or refer to them when designing your journal.

Take your journal with you every day and use any spare time to update your lists and plans.

1 PLAN YOUR WEEK
Write down which days you're eating out and when you're eating in.

2 CHOOSE YOUR RECIPES
Always have ingredients on hand for one recipe you can make with what's in your pantry in case you decide to eat at home.

3 MAKE YOUR SHOPPING LIST
If your plans are always changing, don't buy meat and fish when you do your shopping for the week.

Money Saver

Food is one of the biggest expenses in the home, and most people could eat better and spend less with a little money management. Planning is the key, and your journal is the tool to use.

If you keep a household budget in your journal, you can allocate a certain amount to your weekly groceries. Doing this can be as simple as leaving a section at the bottom of your weekly meal planner and shopping list for your food budget. Then just jot down exactly how much you want to spend on groceries during the week and how much you actually spent. If you were under, great! If you went over, take a second to look at your receipts to see what you could do better next time and write it in your journal. Once you do this for a while, staying on budget will become second nature. Thank you, journal!

Don't forget to keep track of how much you spend on eating out. It's no secret that preparing your own meals is a lot cheaper than dining out or ordering in. You (and your wallet) will be much happier if you cook for yourself. Seriously, you'll enjoy that Cashew Chicken (page 60) so much more if you take the time to make it on your own. Not only will you save a ton of money, you'll also know exactly what you're eating and can feel good about it. If you find that you're reaching for that takeout menu twice a week, I always recommend you look ahead. Pinpoint the busiest day of the week—when you know you'll be tempted to order in—and plan a delicious meal that evening. Be sure to note the name of the dish and everything you need to buy for it in your Weekly Meal Planner and Shopping List, and you'll have no excuse to stray from your menu plans. Alternatively, look in the Cook Now, Eat Later chapter (page 64) for meals you can make in advance. Again, note the recipe and the ingredients you need in your journal, and when you plan to cook it. Then you'll have something homemade ready to reheat when you return.

HABIT TRACKERS

Do you want to make sure you're drinking enough water? Or cut down on the amount of meat or sugary snacks you eat? Perhaps there's a goal you want to achieve? You can use your journal to track your habits and reach your targets, whether you want to monitor habits daily, weekly, or monthly. This visual representation of where your time, money, and energy are going is a great way to keep yourself on the right path.

Use the Habit Tracker template on page 150 to help you keep an eye on any habit you want to maintain, including:

- Days you drank eight 8-ounce (225 ml) glasses of water
- Days you ate five or more portions of fruit and vegetables
- Days you didn't reach for sugary snacks and ate low-calorie meals
- Days you do not order takeout or eat out but cook at home instead
- Days you use up leftovers
- Alcohol-free days
- Days you take lunch to work
- Meat-free days

Waste Less

Food waste is a massive problem today. According to the Natural Resources Defense Council, up to 40 percent of the food in America never gets eaten. If you know that you can buy a week's worth of meat at one time and use it up before it goes bad, go for it. But if you've let that "Best By" date pass you by one too many times, pick up your meat the day before or the day that you need it. Large bags of of vegetables such as carrots may be good value, but there may be more than you can eat in a week. Before creating your weekly shopping list, make a list of the foods in your fridge and pantry that need to be used and then look for suitable recipes. Check The Zero-Waste Kitchen chapter (page 96) for recipes that will inspire you to cook with an ingredient or for ways to preserve excess items to use later. You could also separate your pantry grocery list from your perishable list so that you can shop for them at different times.

Making the Transition

I'm sure you already use some form of note-taking with an app on your phone, a planner, or simply the sticky pads that are all over your house. Whatever you're currently using, it's easy to transition to a simple journaling system. First, figure out what already works for you. If you love the basic list style of your phone's notes app, adopt that format for your journal. It can be tempting to go overboard on creativity when you start a new journal, but if that's not what's functional for you, stick with the basics. If you're unsure what sort of layout you want, try it with a pencil first. Test it out for a couple of days before you decide on what you like and then finalize it. The great thing about journaling is that you can go month to month and change what didn't work. If you're already using a fancy planner, you'll find a lot of great ideas within its pages. While there may be sections that you don't find useful, there'll also be parts that are extremely helpful. Don't be afraid to mimic those in your new journal!

Sticky notes look disorganized, but because you can move them from place to place, they are great for journalers. Once you have your layout built for meal planning, use a sticky note to write down which recipe you would like to make on which day. If your plans change throughout the week, just swap the notes rather than drawing a line through your text.

Making the Most of What You Have

You're sure to learn a lot about yourself as you begin using your journal in the kitchen. You'll notice which proteins you reach for the most, which products you use up quickly, and which ones you probably won't repurchase. As you gain these insights, you can use them to your advantage to prep even more. If you love poultry, start your week off right by roasting a chicken over the weekend. You can then sit down with your journal and plan your meals around it, saving time and money. Maybe you'll use it to add protein to a Super Soup (page 98) one day, mix up a couple of Greek Chicken Salad Pitas (page 111) later in the week, or substitute it for the beef in Beef Pho (page 61). Don't be afraid to adapt the recipes to use what's available.

PANTRY

Soy sauce
Pasta
All-purpose flour
Olive oil

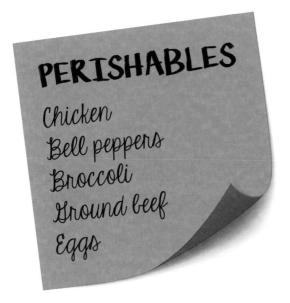

PERISHABLES

Chicken
Bell peppers
Broccoli
Ground beef
Eggs

STARTING A JOURNAL

- Be inspired by your favorite app or planner.
- Try out different styles to find the best one for you.
- Use a pencil to sketch your layout first if you aren't sure it will work.
- Try using sticky notes—the ultimate in flexible organization.

MEAL PLAN: JULY 4-10

MONDAY: KALE GREEK SALAD
WITH TUNA

TUESDAY: SHAKSHUKA

WEDNESDAY: AHI TUNA BURGERS
+ SALAD

THURSDAY: FISH + TOMATOES + POTATO PUFFS

FRIDAY: OUT

SATURDAY: PORK CHOPS + SWISS CHARD
+ MASHED SWEET POTATOES

SUNDAY: TOFU SUSHI BOWLS

BREAKFAST
· EGGS
· SWISS CHARD
· SWEET POTATO

LUNCH
· LEFTOVERS

SNACKS
· PISTACHIOS
· BANANAS
· HB EGGS

produce
· LIMES
· CILANTRO
· GINGER
· AVOCADOS
☆ · CARROTS
☆ · CANTELOUP
☆ · BLUEBERRI
· SWEET POTA
· CUCUMBE
· GARLIC
· SWISS CHA
· PISTACHIO
· BANANA

grocery
· SRIRACHK
· BLACK OL
☆ · CANNED T
☆ · FETA CHEE

BUDGET: $

Use your journal to plan your meals and grocery shopping, and track your spending. It's a great way to save money.

WHICH JOURNAL SHOULD I USE?

Once you have decided to start journaling, you need to choose a journal. You may have seen a suitable notebook and already started planning with it. Or you may have looked in the store and been overwhelmed by all the choices. Here are some things you should think about before you buy. Remember, no matter how beautiful the notebook is, it must be functional or you won't use it.

- **SIZE:** Many successful journalers carry their journal around with them. If you're going to do this, you need a notebook that fits in your purse and won't weigh you down.

- **PAPER WEIGHT:** If you plan to write with a ballpoint pen, you can probably use any type of paper. But if you enjoy writing with a fountain pen or want to decorate the pages of your journal using calligraphy markers or felt-tip pens, look for a journal with thick paper that won't allow the ink to bleed through to the other side.

- **PAPER PATTERN:** Journals are made using blank, lined, squared, or dotted paper. Think about how you want to design your pages. If you're going to use lots of boxes and grids, then squared or dotted paper will form a useful framework for your designs. For a journal that will consist of simple lists, lined paper will be ideal. Or you may want the freedom of blank pages that allow your creativity to flow.

- **BINDING:** Creating a journal is easiest when the book opens out flat. Hardcovers will protect your journal and make it easier to write in, but if you're worried about carrying a heavy book around with you, try a paperback instead. Many people choose journals with sewn bindings, but you may prefer a spiral-bound book.

- **EXTRAS:** An elastic or clasp closure will keep your journal closed to protect the pages and any loose papers stored inside. A pen loop attached to the cover will mean you always have a pen on hand. Ribbon bookmarks will help you to find the pages you use the most.

"A place for everything,
and everything in its place."

–Isabella Beeton

2

GET ORGANIZED

When it comes to feeding yourself during the week, ordering takeout or meeting friends for a quick dinner often seems like the easiest thing to do. Instead of shelling out unnecessary cash, use the organization strategies in this chapter with your journal to plan ahead, and you'll discover the key to dinner success that you've been looking for.

There is a time and place for having someone else prepare your meals, but cooking for yourself is usually healthier, cheaper, and yes, even quicker. My hope is that this section inspires you to get out your new pens and start plotting out meal plans and grocery lists for the weeks ahead—not because you feel like it's the right thing to do, but because you're excited about taking control of what you eat.

Plan Ahead

If you're someone who makes multiple grocery store visits each week, you may think it'll be impossible to shop just once a week. With the help of meal planning and functional shopping lists, you can do it! You'll save time throughout the week and also avoid any unnecessary purchases (looking at you, candy bars!).

The first step to shopping success is to decide what you want to eat throughout the week. Sure, the occasional craving may come up, but for the most part, you can preplan your meals and then proceed to make a shopping list for the week. Look at the current contents of your fridge and pantry to see what you can use, then go from there to build your list in your journal.

You've probably heard that you shouldn't grocery shop on an empty stomach, and that couldn't be more true. Just by reaching for a healthy snack before you head into the store, you're ensuring that you're not grabbing every new snack from the end caps to ease your hunger pangs.

Set aside some time on the weekend to PLAN YOUR MEALS and write a SHOPPING LIST for the week ahead.

SHOPPING LIST TIPS

Planning ahead can help to make your list—and shopping—more efficient.

- Add staple items to your shopping list as soon as you know you're about to run out—you'll never be without flour, rice, pasta, or oil again.

- Make meal planning easy by assigning each night of the week a theme. Think, "Taco Tuesday" or "Pizza Friday."

- Organize your meals according to what's on sale. Go through your store's weekly ad before shopping and use it for inspiration and budgeting.

- Start with one main recipe for the week and build the rest of your meals from leftover ingredients.

- Don't let the price of broccoli or lack of lentils at the grocery store derail your meal plan. Add a few ingredient alternatives to your shopping list just in case something is more expensive than expected or out-of-stock.

- Check "use by" dates as you shop and choose items that will last as long as possible.

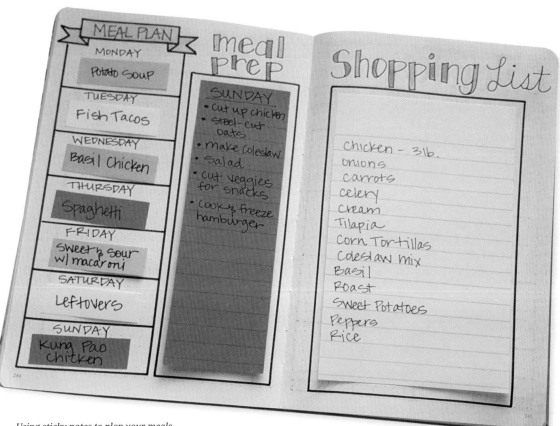

Using sticky notes to plan your meals allows you to move things around so you can keep your menu for the week flexible.

In the digital era, there are multiple options for grocery shopping. Whether you want to order online and have your groceries delivered, or arrange to have them ready for you to pick up at the store, you no longer have to scour the aisles yourself to find what you need. While there may be an extra cost for having someone else do your shopping, the upcharge is nothing compared to the price of impulse purchases you'd probably make in the store. And you can see how much you're spending as you shop.

Try it out! To start being more organized with your meals, use the shopping list template on page 140 or make a copy of it in your journal. While flipping through the book, make a list of the dishes that you want to prepare and create a shopping list of the ingredients you need.

A Meal from the Pantry

We all have those nights when there's no way we can get to the store and need to forage for dinner in your pantry and fridge. As long as you have a few staple ingredients on standby, you can make a dinner-party-worthy meal with little effort.

Canned goods are among the most important items to keep in your pantry. Beans can provide a vegetarian protein option, tuna is affordable and delicious, and tomatoes make a magnificent marinara in no time. Frozen vegetables like corn, broccoli, and peas are packaged at their peak ripeness and will lend nutrition and flavor to your weeknight fare. Dried pastas, rice, and quinoa are essential for a well-rounded meal, and fried eggs can be the savory cherry on top of just about any dish.

Last-Minute Buys

Sometimes it might not be practical to pick up certain items on your weekly shopping trip: some perishable ingredients might go bad before you get a chance to use them. While I want to streamline your grocery shopping process, I also want to make sure you're cutting down on food waste and making the most of the food you buy. Meats and certain vegetables have a shorter shelf life than other items on your list, so popping into the store to pick those up at the last minute may be the smart way to go.

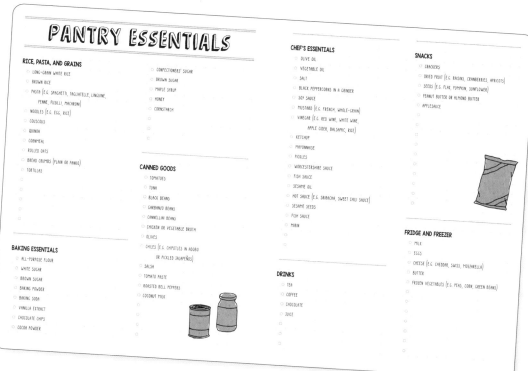

PANTRY ESSENTIALS

RICE, PASTA, AND GRAINS

- ○ LONG-GRAIN WHITE RICE
- ○ BROWN RICE
- ○ PASTA (E.G. SPAGHETTI, TAGLIATELLE, LINGUINE, PENNE, FUSILLI, MACARONI)
- ○ NOODLES (E.G. EGG, RICE)
- ○ COUSCOUS
- ○ QUINOA
- ○ CORNMEAL
- ○ ROLLED OATS
- ○ BREAD CRUMBS (PLAIN OR PANKO)
- ○ TORTILLAS
- ○
- ○
- ○
- ○

BAKING ESSENTIALS

- ○ ALL-PURPOSE FLOUR
- ○ WHITE SUGAR
- ○ BROWN SUGAR
- ○ BAKING POWDER
- ○ BAKING SODA
- ○ VANILLA EXTRACT
- ○ CHOCOLATE CHIPS
- ○ COCOA POWDER

- ○ CONFECTIONERS' SUGAR
- ○ BROWN SUGAR
- ○ MAPLE SYRUP
- ○ HONEY
- ○ CORNSTARCH
- ○
- ○
- ○

CANNED GOODS

- ○ TOMATOES
- ○ TUNA
- ○ BLACK BEANS
- ○ GARBANZO BEANS
- ○ CANNELLINI BEANS
- ○ CHICKEN OR VEGETABLE BROTH
- ○ OLIVES
- ○ CHILES (E.G. CHIPOTLES IN ADOBO OR PICKLED JALAPEÑOS)
- ○ SALSA
- ○ TOMATO PASTE
- ○ ROASTED BELL PEPPERS
- ○ COCONUT MILK
- ○
- ○
- ○
- ○

CHEF'S ESSENTIALS

- ○ OLIVE OIL
- ○ VEGETABLE OIL
- ○ SALT
- ○ BLACK PEPPERCORNS IN A GRINDER
- ○ SOY SAUCE
- ○ MUSTARD (E.G. FRENCH, WHOLE-GRAIN)
- ○ VINEGAR (E.G. RED WINE, WHITE WINE, APPLE CIDER, BALSAMIC, RICE)
- ○ KETCHUP
- ○ MAYONNAISE
- ○ PICKLES
- ○ WORCESTERSHIRE SAUCE
- ○ FISH SAUCE
- ○ SESAME OIL
- ○ HOT SAUCE (E.G. SRIRACHA, SWEET CHILI SAUCE)
- ○ SESAME SEEDS
- ○ FISH SAUCE
- ○ MIRIN
- ○
- ○

DRINKS

- ○ TEA
- ○ COFFEE
- ○ CHOCOLATE
- ○ JUICE
- ○
- ○
- ○
- ○
- ○

SNACKS

- ○ CRACKERS
- ○ DRIED FRUIT (E.G. RAISINS, CRANBERRIES, APRICOTS)
- ○ SEEDS (E.G. FLAX, PUMPKIN, SUNFLOWER)
- ○ PEANUT BUTTER OR ALMOND BUTTER
- ○ APPLESAUCE
- ○
- ○
- ○
- ○

FRIDGE AND FREEZER

- ○ MILK
- ○ EGGS
- ○ CHEESE (E.G. CHEDDAR, SWISS, MOZZARELLA)
- ○ BUTTER
- ○ FROZEN VEGETABLES (E.G. PEAS, CORN, GREEN BEANS)
- ○
- ○
- ○

Use a Pantry Essentials template like the example on page 138 as the basis for your weekly shopping list.

MONEY-SAVING TIPS

There are many things you can do to save pennies without making life complicated. Here are some of my favorites.

- Buy whole vegetables rather than prechopped ones and prepare them yourself.

- Whole heads of romaine and iceberg lettuce keep longer in the fridge than bags of washed salad. Little gem lettuces are perfect if you're cooking for one.

- Use up your leftovers (see The Zero-Waste Kitchen, page 96).

- Freeze leftover broth and wine in ice-cube trays and store until you need them. Add the frozen cubes to sauces as they cook, and they'll add flavor as they defrost. As a general rule, one cube contains about 2 tablespoons of liquid.

- Invest in some airtight storage boxes—they'll help food last longer.

- If you have space in your freezer, buy meat and fish when they are on sale. Store them until needed, but for no more than three months.

The "Magic Box"

Spices and condiments will add flavor to any recipe, but how do you know which ones will taste good together? If you're following a recipe, the work is done for you. But, if you want to experiment in the kitchen, the rules can get a little blurry! When your pantry is stocked with these herbs, spices, and sauces, you can mix and match within each flavor family to create an original dish of your own invention.

SWEET
Cinnamon
Allspice
Ginger
Cloves
Nutmeg
Vanilla

MEXICAN
Chili powder
Cumin
Chipotle
Paprika
Taco seasoning

INDIAN
Coriander
Cumin
Turmeric
Garam masala
Cayenne pepper
Curry powder

ASIAN
Five spice
Sichuan pepper
Star anise
Red pepper flakes

MEDITERRANEAN
Oregano
Thyme
Rosemary
Parsley
Basil
Dill
Saffron

SPICES and DRIED HERBS don't stay fresh forever. While it may appear cheaper to buy them in bulk, it may prove MORE EXPENSIVE in the long term if you cannot use them up before they lose their flavor.

HOT SAUCES

Sriracha Spicy Sriracha's recent popularity is for good reason. Its hot and tangy flavor means that you can use it to dress up everything from pho to burgers with ease.

Harissa Thanks to its unique blend of chili peppers, the smoky flavor of harissa is what sets it apart from other spicy condiments.

Wasabi This is so much more than the green smear on the side of your sushi plate. Mix wasabi with mayo to lessen the punch and make a delicious spread for your sandwich.

Sweet Chili Sauce If your taste buds are more accustomed to sweet rather than spicy, then a mellow sweet chili sauce is the perfect addition to your stir-fry.

Gochujang This spicy Korean fermented condiment is made from chili powder, glutinous rice, fermented soybean, barley malt powder, and salt. Add it to your next bowl of bibimbap.

Horseradish Your prime rib roast isn't complete without a spoonful or two of pungent horseradish sauce. Look online for advice on how to turn prepared horseradish into a tasty sauce.

Tabasco Pepper Sauce You can't go wrong with this classic hot sauce. Containing tabasco peppers, vinegar, and salt, it'll add spice without competing with the other flavors of your dish.

Piri-piri If you're looking for a well-rounded hot sauce that'll bring a bright lemon-forward flavor to any dish, African piri-piri will be your new best friend.

Sambal This Indonesian favorite is a paste made up of ground chili peppers, shallots, garlic, and, most importantly, shrimp paste.

Equipment

You don't need high-end cookware from an upscale store to create delicious, simple, and healthy meals. As long as you have these basic tools, you'll be able to master any of the recipes in this book without making your cabinets overflow and maxing out your credit card. Use the template on page 136 to start a list of tools you want to add to your kitchen.

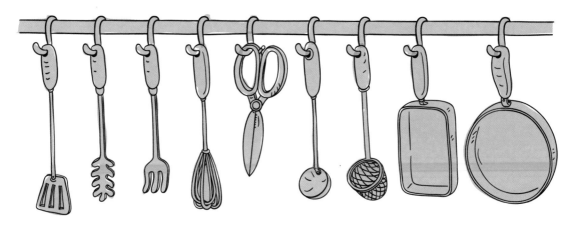

○ CHEF'S KNIFE
Go for an 8-inch (20 cm) knife so that you can use it for cutting meat and poultry, as well as vegetables and herbs.

○ PARING KNIFE
Choose a paring knife with a heavier blade to make mundane tasks like peeling potatoes much easier.

○ CUTTING BOARD
Pick up a plastic board that can be washed in the dishwasher.

○ SLOW COOKER
Be sure to find a slow cooker with a ceramic or porcelain removable insert, glass lid, and multiple heat settings. A 3- to 4-quart (2.8 to 3.8 L) cooker is perfect for small households, while a 6-quart (5.7 L) cooker is ideal for four people or more.

○ BLENDER
Investing in a high-powered blender (1,000–1,560 watts) will ensure that all of your smoothies and soups come out perfect every time.

○ CAN OPENER
It might be tempting to splurge on an electric can opener, but a good-quality handheld one will yield the same results.

○ COLANDER
Whether you're draining pasta or cleaning lettuce, a large, durable, heat-resistant colander is a must.

○ TONGS
A set of stainless steel locking tongs will save valuable storage space in your utensil drawer and provide a better grip for your food.

○ WOODEN SPOON
A beech or maple wooden spoon with a flat head will stand the test of time and provide all the stirring and scraping capabilities you need.

○ MEASURING CUPS

Opt for a set of measuring cups with a handle and a spout so that you can easily pour out wet and dry contents. A clear set is even better— you'll be able to read the measurements from the side.

○ WHISK

A standard wire balloon whisk will see you through many batches of scrambled eggs and whipped cream.

○ MEASURING SPOONS

Make sure that the set you choose goes from 1 tablespoon to ⅛ teaspoon, especially if you're often cooking for one.

○ PIE DISH

An 8- or 9-inch (20 or 22 cm) glass pie dish will heat slowly and evenly, yielding a beautiful quiche or pot pie every time.

○ CAST IRON SKILLET

A good 10¼-inch (26 cm) cast iron skillet will last you generations. Your best bet is to look in flea markets for a previously loved and well-seasoned skillet at a great price!

○ LARGE NONSTICK SKILLET

By far the most-used kitchen tool in your arsenal will be a nonstick skillet. Look for a ceramic-coated or hard anodized one.

○ MEDIUM SAUCEPAN

A 1½-quart (1.4 L) stainless steel saucepan is a versatile option that you can move from the stove to the oven with ease.

○ LARGE POT

A large pot is necessary for all those stews and pastas you'll be making. Keep your eyes peeled for one that has high sides and a thick, heavy bottom.

○ LOAF PAN

Stoneware can be too fragile for the beginner baker. When selecting your perfect loaf pan, reach for glass, metal, or nonstick to make your favorite banana bread.

○ BAKING SHEET

Baking sheets come in many sizes, so choose what works best for your household. A quarter sheet pan would be ideal for a home of one or two people, and a half sheet pan would be fine for a house of two to four people.

○ POT HOLDERS

You certainly don't want any burn accidents in the kitchen! Opt for pot holders that have a silicone grip so you can avoid dropping that hot pot of stew.

○ PIZZA PAN

A nonstick 15¾-inch (40 cm) pizza pan with perforations will allow your crust to cook evenly while remaining crisp.

○ RUBBER SPATULA

Select a spatula that's molded from silicone from the handle to the tip for easy clean-up.

○ MIXING BOWLS

Stainless steel mixing bowls won't absorb odors and flavors like plastic, so you can use them for both savory and sweet recipes.

TIME-SAVING EXTRAS

○ **Vegetable Peeler:**
Use in place of a paring knife to peel vegetables.

○ **Kitchen Shears:**
For when you need to trim herbs or spatchcock a chicken.

○ **Garlic Press:**
Keep your hands and cutting board free from any garlic smells.

○ **Kitchen Scale:**
Enables accurate measuring.

○ **Meat Thermometer:**
Ensure your meats are cooked to the perfect temperature.

PART 2

RECIPES
FOR
JOURNALERS

"Good food is
the foundation
of genuine
happiness."

–Auguste Escoffier

3

THE RECIPES

Now that you know why you should be journaling and how to get organized, it's time to jump into the recipes! The dishes in the following chapters are my favorite kind: simple, fuss-free, and most importantly absolutely delicious. There are simple meals that can be on the table in just 10 or 20 minutes, takeout favorites, meal-prep batch recipes, one-pot wonders, and showstoppers for entertaining. The recipes are the perfect way to start your journaling journey. I've included some of my absolute favorite classics, like Swedish Meatballs with Pasta (page 56) and Chicken Cacciatore (page 70), along with unique dishes like Chicken Cordon Bleu Burgers (page 50). You'll find that many of the recipes use minimal equipment and contain the same ingredients so that you can use leftovers to create multiple meals throughout the week. Once you've stocked your pantry and perfected your grocery lists, you'll be a regular wiz at getting dinner on the table—fast!

FASTER THAN READING A MENU

In the time it takes you to scour the menu and figure out what you want to order, you can make dinner at home in 15 minutes or less with one of these five recipes.

Thai Broccoli Salad

SERVES : 2
PREPARATION TIME : 12 MINUTES

This healthy vegan salad will having you putting away that Thai takeout menu in a hurry. It keeps well in the fridge, so double the recipe and take it for lunch!

SHOPPING LIST

For the Spicy Peanut Dressing

O 1½ tsp. peanut butter

O ¼ to ¾ tsp. Sriracha

O 1½ tbsp. soy sauce

O 1½ tsp. rice vinegar

O ¼ tsp. sesame oil

O ¼ tsp. freshly squeezed lime juice

O ¼ tsp. grated fresh ginger

O 1 small garlic clove, minced

For the Salad

O 2 cups (350 g) broccoli florets

O 1 medium carrot, peeled and chopped into matchsticks

O ½ red bell pepper, seeded and thinly sliced

O ⅓ cup (65 g) frozen shelled edamame, thawed

O 2 or 3 green onions, sliced

O ⅓ cup (12 g) coarsely chopped fresh cilantro

O ¼ cup (35 g) roasted peanuts

O 1 tsp. sesame seeds

1. To make the dressing, whisk the peanut butter, Sriracha, soy sauce, rice vinegar, sesame oil, lime juice, ginger, and garlic together until combined. If it seems too thick, add water 1 teaspoon at a time. Set aside.

2. Combine the broccoli, carrot, pepper, edamame, onions, cilantro, peanuts, and sesame seeds in a large bowl. Drizzle with the dressing and toss thoroughly, making make sure the veggies are completed coated.

3. Serve immediately, or refrigerate until ready to serve.

TIP: Don't be afraid to get some help from the grocery store when it comes to chopping the vegetables. Precut broccoli florets are a great time-saver, and ½ cup of packaged shredded carrots can be used in place of the whole carrot.

NOTES

Garlic Shrimp with Rice

SERVES : 2
PREPARATION TIME : 2 MINUTES
COOKING TIME : 8 MINUTES

Shrimp are one of the quickest-cooking proteins—especially if you buy them peeled and deveined. This recipe is bound to become a Saturday night favorite in your house.

SHOPPING LIST

- ½ cup (125 g) rice
- 2 tsp. olive oil
- 2 tbsp. unsalted butter
- ½ lb. (225 g) raw medium shrimp, peeled and deveined
- ½ tsp. salt
- ¼ tsp. ground black pepper
- 2 garlic cloves, finely chopped
- ½ tsp. Italian seasoning
- Pinch of red pepper flakes
- 2 tsp. lemon juice
- 2 tbsp. white wine (or chicken broth)
- Salt and ground black pepper, to taste
- 2 tbsp. chopped fresh parsley, to garnish
- Quarter slices of lemon, to garnish

NOTES

....
....
....
....
....
....
....
....

1. Cook the rice following the instructions on page 113.

2. Meanwhile, heat the olive oil and 1 tablespoon of the butter in a medium skillet over medium-high heat. Arrange the shrimp in one layer and sprinkle with the salt and pepper. Cook for 1 minute without stirring, so that the bottoms of the shrimp are slightly browned.

3. Stir in the garlic, Italian seasoning, and red pepper flakes and flip the shrimp over. Cook for another minute or two. Transfer the shrimp to a plate and keep warm.

4. Add the remaining butter, the lemon juice, and wine to the pan and stir. Bring the sauce to a simmer for 2 to 3 minutes, stirring regularly until it starts to thicken.

5. Drain the rice and toss to coat with the sauce. Serve alongside the shrimp, garnished with the parsley and lemon slices.

TIP: You can use frozen shrimp instead of fresh. Just cook them for an additional 2 minutes until they're pink and opaque.

Grilled Cheese with Apple

SERVES : 2
PREPARATION TIME : 5 MINUTES
COOKING TIME : 8 MINUTES

There's a reason why you used to get so excited when your mom whipped up a grilled cheese sandwich. Now you can get that same comforting feeling for yourself.

SHOPPING LIST

- 4 slices multigrain bread, ½-inch (1.2 cm) thick
- 1 cup (80 g) shredded white Cheddar cheese, at room temperature
- 1 small Granny Smith apple, peeled, cored, and sliced thinly
- 4 or 5 kale leaves, rinsed and torn into pieces
- 2 tbsp. unsalted butter, at room temperature

NOTES

....
....
....
....
....
....
....
....
....
....
....
....
....
....

1. Divide half the cheese between two slices of bread and arrange the apple slices and kale on top. Top with the remaining cheese, then the remaining slices of bread. Spread the outside of each sandwich with butter, using ½ tablespoon of butter for each slice of bread.

2. Heat a large nonstick skillet over medium heat. Add the sandwiches and cook for 3 to 4 minutes on each side, pressing down with a spatula to flatten the sandwiches, until the bread is golden brown and the cheese has melted. Keep an eye on the bread. If it starts to burn before the cheese melts, lower the heat. Serve immediately.

TIP: Nothing goes better with a grilled cheese than tomato soup. Make sure that you have a can on hand, or try the Roasted Tomato-Basil Soup on page 105!

Cheese Omelette with Tomato Salad

SERVES : 2
PREPARATION TIME : 10 MINUTES
COOKING TIME : 5 MINUTES

There's no need to be intimidated—you can make the perfect omelette. If you can scramble eggs, then you can ace this breakfast-for-dinner with ease.

SHOPPING LIST

For the Omelette

- O 4 large eggs
- O ¼ tsp. salt
- O ¼ tsp. ground black pepper
- O 1 tbsp. olive oil
- O ¼ cup (20 g) shredded Cheddar cheese

For the Tomato Salad

- O 2 cups (320 g) cherry tomatoes, halved
- O ½ tsp. salt
- O ¼ tsp. ground black pepper
- O 1½ tbsp. olive oil
- O 2 tbsp. finely chopped red onion
- O 2 tbsp. finely chopped flat-leaf parsley
- O 2 slices bread of your choice, to serve

NOTES

....
....
....
....
....
....
....
....

1. Add the eggs, salt, and pepper to a medium mixing bowl, and whisk until combined.

2. Heat the olive oil in a small nonstick skillet over low heat. Carefully pour in half of the eggs. Tilt the pan to spread them out evenly, swirling the eggs around the pan a little. Cook the omelette for 1 to 2 minutes, until it begins to firm up on the bottom and the sides, but is still a little wet on top. Sprinkle the cheese on top of the omelette.

3. Using a spatula, lift the edges of the omelette, then fold it in half. Cook for an additional 30 seconds to allow the cheese to melt. Remove the omelette from the pan and repeat the process with the rest of the eggs.

4. To make the salad, toss the tomatoes with the salt, pepper, olive oil, red onion, and chopped parsley. Serve the omelette with the tomato salad and a slice of bread.

Pesto & Pea Tagliatelle

SERVES : 2
PREPARATION TIME : 8 MINUTES
COOKING TIME : 7 MINUTES

For those times when you need a speedy last-minute date-night meal, this fresh and impressive pasta dish is the way to go. Serve it with an arugula salad.

SHOPPING LIST

- 4 oz. (115 g) tagliatelle
- ½ cup (60 g) frozen peas
- 2 cups (40 g) fresh baby arugula
- 2 tbsp. grated Parmesan cheese
- 2 tsp. olive oil
- 2 tsp. lemon juice
- ¼ tsp. ground black pepper
- 2 tbsp. prepared pesto
- 2 tbsp. thinly sliced fresh basil leaves
- ½ tsp. lemon zest
- ½ tsp. salt

NOTES

....
....
....
....
....
....
....
....
....
....
....
....

1. Bring a large pot of water to a boil and cook the tagliatelle according to the package instructions, about 7 minutes. Two minutes before the pasta is finished cooking, add the peas to the pot.

2. While the pasta is cooking, put the arugula and 1 tablespoon of the Parmesan into a large mixing bowl. Drizzle evenly with the olive oil and lemon juice, and sprinkle with the black pepper. Toss until combined.

3. Drain the pasta and peas in a strainer and return them to the warm pot. Add the pesto, fresh basil, lemon zest, salt, and the remaining Parmesan. Serve immediately with the arugula salad.

TIP: Reserve some of the cooking water, and if the sauce looks thick, add up to 3 tablespoons of water to dilute it.

FASTER THAN PHONING

When the recipes take only 30 minutes or less to cook, there's no reason to order in. The following dishes combine classic recipes with a few modern twists.

Crispy Tofu Sushi Bowl

SERVES : 2
PREPARATION TIME : 20 MINUTES
COOKING TIME : 10 MINUTES

You don't have to dine out to eat sushi. Grab some sake and have fun at home creating your own vegetarian sushi bowl complete with crispy tofu.

SHOPPING LIST

- ½ cup (125 g) rice
- 1½ tbsp. mirin
- 1 tbsp. soy sauce
- 1 tsp. sugar
- 1¼ tsp. rice vinegar
- ½ tsp. grated fresh ginger
- ¼ tsp. sesame oil
- ⅔ cup (140 g) extra-firm tofu, drained and cubed
- 1 small sheet toasted nori, broken up into pieces
- ½ medium avocado, pitted, peeled, and finely diced
- ¼ medium English cucumber, halved and sliced
- ½ medium carrot, coarsely grated
- Sesame seeds, to garnish

1. Cook the rice following the instructions on page 113.

2. Meanwhile, combine the mirin, soy sauce, sugar, ¼ teaspoon of the rice vinegar, ginger, and sesame oil in a shallow bowl. Add the tofu and toss to coat. Marinate for 10 minutes, stirring twice.

3. Drain the rice, refresh by rinsing with cold water, and drain again. Add the remaining 1 tablespoon rice vinegar to the cooked rice and toss to combine. Divide the rice between two bowls. Add the nori pieces, avocado, cucumber, and carrot.

4. Heat a large nonstick skillet over medium-high heat. Add the tofu and marinade, and cook for 5 to 7 minutes, turning gently, until the tofu cubes are browned and crisp. Divide them between the two bowls and chill in the fridge for 10 minutes. Garnish with the sesame seeds and serve.

TIPS: Have a favorite sushi roll? Don't be afraid to get creative and try it at home. Add ¾ cup (125 g) imitation crab meat and a drizzle of Sriracha mayo to your bowl to mimic a yummy California roll. Add an extra flavor dimension by serving some wasabi on the side.

NOTES

....
....
....

Linguine with Lemon Sauce

SERVES : 2
PREPARATION TIME : 5 MINUTES
COOKING TIME : 15 MINUTES

At the end of a long day, there's something comforting about a bowl of creamy carbs. You'll probably find all the ingredients you need in your pantry.

SHOPPING LIST

- 4 oz. (115 g) linguine
- ¼ cup (60 g) unsalted butter
- 2 garlic cloves, minced
- 2 tbsp. lemon juice
- Zest of ½ lemon
- 2 tbsp. heavy cream
- 3 tbsp. pasta cooking water
- ¼ cup (10 g) grated Parmesan cheese, plus extra to serve, if desired
- ½ tsp. salt
- ¼ tsp. ground black pepper
- 1 tbsp. finely chopped parsley, to garnish

NOTES

....
....
....
....
....
....
....
....
....
....
....
....

1. Cook the linguine for 2 minutes less than stated in the package instructions.

2. While the pasta is cooking, melt the butter in a medium skillet over medium heat. Add the garlic and cook for 2 minutes, stirring occasionally, until the garlic is softened and fragrant.

3. Stir in the lemon juice and zest, cream, and 3 tablespoons of the pasta cooking water. Simmer for 2 minutes, until combined.

4. Drain the cooked pasta, add it to the skillet, and stir to combine. Cook for an additional minute to allow the pasta to soak up some of the sauce. Stir in the cheese and season with the salt and pepper. Serve immediately garnished with the parsley, with extra Parmesan cheese, if desired.

TIP: This recipe is meat-free but, if you'd like some protein, try adding ¾ cup (250 g) peeled and deveined shrimp to the skillet in step 2, cooking for 4 minutes, or until the shrimp are just pink. Take care not to overcook them.

Sun-Dried Tomato Gnocchi

SERVES : 2
PREPARATION TIME : 3 MINUTES
COOKING TIME : 12 MINUTES

Delicious meals often take just a few ingredients. This creamy gnocchi uses a handful of items and may just make you feel like you're in the foothills of Tuscany.

SHOPPING LIST

- O 16-oz. (454 g) package potato gnocchi
- O 1 tbsp. olive oil from a jar of sun-dried tomatoes (see below)
- O 3 garlic cloves, minced
- O ¼ cup (65 g) sun-dried tomatoes in olive oil, drained and minced
- O ½ cup (120 ml) whipping cream
- O ½ tsp. salt
- O ¼ tsp. ground black pepper
- O 2 tbsp. grated Parmesan cheese

NOTES

....
....
....
....
....
....
....
....
....
....
....
....

1. Bring a large pot of water to a boil, and cook the gnocchi according to the package instructions.

2. While the gnocchi are cooking, heat the olive oil in a medium skillet over medium-low heat. Add the garlic and cook for 1 minute, stirring occasionally, until the garlic is softened and fragrant. Add the sun-dried tomatoes and stir to combine.

3. Add the cream, salt, and pepper to the skillet and cook for 5 minutes, until the sauce is creamy and will coat the gnocchi.

4. Once the gnocchi are cooked, drain and add to the skillet, mixing thoroughly. Top with the grated Parmesan cheese, and serve immediately.

TIP: This dish is great with sautéed mushrooms and spinach! Add ¾ cup (110 g) sliced mushrooms after you add the garlic in step 2 and sauté for 5 minutes, or until the mushrooms are browned. Then add 1 cup (100 g) baby spinach leaves and sauté for 1 to 2 minutes, or until the spinach is wilted.

Shakshuka

SERVES : 2
PREPARATION TIME : 3 MINUTES
COOKING TIME : 20 MINUTES

Eggs are always a good idea, especially when they're bathed in a tomato sauce. Whether you're making this for brunch or dinner, it's a winner every time.

SHOPPING LIST

- O 1 tbsp. olive oil
- O 2 garlic cloves, minced
- O ½ small jalapeño pepper, seeded and sliced
- O 14-oz. (400 g) can diced tomatoes
- O ½ tsp. cumin
- O ¾ tsp. paprika
- O ½ tsp. salt
- O ¼ tsp. ground black pepper
- O 1 tsp. tomato paste
- O 4 eggs
- O 2 tbsp. crumbled feta cheese, to garnish
- O 1 tbsp. finely chopped parsley, to garnish

NOTES

....
....
....
....
....
....
....
....
....
....
....

1. Heat the olive oil in a small, heavy-bottomed skillet over medium heat. Add the garlic and jalapeño and sauté for 2 minutes, or until the garlic becomes soft and fragrant and the jalapeño softens slightly.

2. Add the tomatoes, cumin, paprika, salt, pepper, and tomato paste to the skillet and stir. Bring to a boil, then reduce the heat and let simmer for 6 minutes, or until the sauce is thickened.

3. Crack the eggs into the tomato sauce. Cook for 5 minutes, or until the eggs are mostly cooked through. Cover the skillet and cook for another 2 minutes to cook the top of the eggs. Check the eggs occasionally to ensure the yolks don't get overcooked.

4. Remove from heat and garnish with the crumbled feta and parsley. Serve immediately.

TIP: No shakshuka is complete without a loaf of crusty bread to soak up that sauce and runny egg yolk. Try serving with torn pieces of naan, pita, or your favorite loaf of bakery-style bread.

Cheesy Black Bean Chilaquiles

SERVES : 2
PREPARATION TIME : 10 MINUTES
COOKING TIME : 20 MINUTES

Have you ever used leftover chips and salsa to create an epic meal that's worthy of company? These vegetarian chilaquiles are a perfect example of how to do it.

SHOPPING LIST

- 2 tbsp. vegetable oil
- ½ large onion, chopped
- 1 cup (225 g) medium salsa
- 2 ripe tomatoes, quartered
- 1 tsp. ground chipotle or chili powder
- 1⅓ cups (215 g) canned black beans, rinsed
- ½ tsp. salt
- ¼ tsp. ground black pepper
- 2 eggs
- 5 cups (625 g) tortilla chips
- ¼ cup (20 g) grated Pepper Jack cheese
- 2 tbsp. finely chopped cilantro, to garnish
- ½ large avocado, diced, to garnish
- ½ lime, cut into wedges, to garnish

NOTES

....
....
....
....
....
....
....
....

1. Heat 1 tablespoon of the vegetable oil in a medium skillet over medium-high heat. Add the onion and cook for 5 minutes, stirring frequently, until softened.

2. Combine the salsa, tomatoes, and chipotle powder in a blender and blend to a purée. Transfer to the skillet, add the beans and cook for 5 minutes, stirring frequently, until warmed through. Season with the salt and pepper.

3. In a separate, nonstick skillet, heat the remaining 1 tablespoon of oil over medium-high heat. Fry the eggs for 3 minutes, or until the whites are just set; season with a pinch of salt and pepper.

4. Stir the tortilla chips into the black bean sauce. Divide between two bowls and sprinkle with the cheese. Top each bowl with an egg. Garnish with the cilantro, avocado, and a lime wedge.

TIP: To make these chilaquiles vegan, omit the eggs and substitute your favorite vegan cheese.

Vegetarian Salade Niçoise

SERVES : 2
PREPARATION TIME : 20 MINUTES
COOKING TIME : 10 MINUTES

Only the heartiest salads are dinner-worthy. This salade Niçoise, bursting with green beans, potatoes, and hard-boiled eggs, fits the bill.

SHOPPING LIST

For the Dressing

- 1 tbsp. lemon juice
- 1 tsp. Dijon mustard
- ¼ cup (60 ml) extra virgin olive oil
- Pinch of salt
- Pinch of ground black pepper

For the Salad

- 8 oz. (225 g) Yukon gold potatoes, sliced in ¼-inch (5 mm) slices
- 1 tsp. white wine vinegar
- 8 oz. (225 g) fresh green beans, ends trimmed
- ⅓ head Bibb lettuce, leaves separated, washed and dried
- ½ cup (80 g) cherry tomatoes, halved
- 3 hard-boiled eggs, peeled, chilled, and halved lengthwise
- ¼ cup (30 g) pitted Niçoise or Kalamata olives

NOTES

....
....
....
....
....

1. To make the dressing, whisk together the lemon juice and mustard. Continue whisking and slowly drizzle in the oil, until the ingredients are fully combined. Whisk in the salt and pepper.

2. Bring a fresh pot of water to a boil. Add the potato slices and cook for 5 minutes, or until just cooked through. Drain, transfer them to a large bowl, and add 1 teaspoon of vinegar. Toss gently and let them cool for 10 minutes.

3. Meanwhile bring a second pot of water to a boil. Drop the beans in and cook for 2 to 3 minutes, until they are just cooked through but still crisp and bright green. Drain and transfer to a bowl of ice water to cool. Drain and pat dry.

4. Line a dish with the lettuce. Arrange the beans, potatoes, tomatoes, eggs, and olives on top. Drizzle half the dressing over the salad, and serve the rest on the side. Serve immediately.

TIP: A classic salade Niçoise is finished with tuna. Do like the French and add a 5-ounce (140 g) can of tuna packed in oil.

Spring Pasta Salad

SERVES : 2
PREPARATION TIME : 15 MINUTES
COOKING TIME : 10 MINUTES

The basil dressing, garden peas, chunks of mozzarella cheese, and slices of fresh peach in this pasta salad are a perfect combination to enjoy on warmer days.

SHOPPING LIST

For the Salad

O 1 cup (115 g) penne pasta

O ½ cup (80 g) cherry tomatoes, quartered

O ¼ cup (30 g) fresh or frozen garden peas, thawed if frozen

O ½ peach, sliced

O 2 tbsp. baby arugula leaves

O 3 oz. (85 g) mozzarella, drained and cubed

For the Dressing

O ½ small shallot

O ½ cup (6 g) fresh basil leaves

O 1 small garlic clove

O ⅛ tsp. red pepper flakes

O 2 tbsp. olive oil

O 1 tbsp. lemon juice

O ½ tsp. salt

NOTES

....
....
....
....
....
....
....
....

1. Place a large pot of water over high heat and bring to a boil. Stir in the pasta. Cook according to the package instructions. Drain the cooked pasta with a colander and rinse with cold water. Shake off the excess water and transfer the pasta to a large serving bowl.

2. Meanwhile, combine the dressing ingredients in a blender and blend on high for 1 minute, or until very smooth. Set aside.

3. Add the tomatoes, peas, peach slices, arugula, and mozzarella cubes to the pasta. Pour the dressing over the top and toss well to coat. Serve immediately or, for a chilled salad, chill for 30 minutes to 1 hour.

TIP: This salad is a great way to use leftover cooked pasta. You will need 2 cups (230 g).

Salmon with Tahini Lemon Sauce

The great thing about fish is how quickly it cooks! This healthy salmon dish only takes 10 minutes in the oven, so you can have dinner on the table ASAP.

SHOPPING LIST

- O 1 tbsp. olive oil
- O 1 tbsp. lemon juice
- O ½ tsp. lemon zest
- O 1½ tsp. Greek yogurt
- O 1 garlic clove, minced
- O ½ tsp. chopped fresh oregano (or 1 pinch dried oregano)
- O ¼ tsp. salt
- O ¼ tsp. ground black pepper
- O 2 salmon fillets (about 12 oz./340 g in total)

For the Sauce

- O ¼ cup (55 g) sesame tahini
- O Zest and juice of 1 lemon
- O 1 garlic clove, minced
- O 1 tbsp. warm water
- O 1 tbsp. red wine vinegar
- O 2 tbsp. extra-virgin olive oil
- O ½ tsp. salt

NOTES

....
....
....
....
....
....
....

1. Preheat the oven to 400°F (200°C).

2. Combine the oil, lemon juice and zest, yogurt, garlic, oregano, salt, and pepper in a shallow bowl. Add the salmon and marinate for 10 minutes.

3. Place the salmon in a baking dish and bake for 10 minutes, or until it just starts to flake easily.

4. While the salmon is cooking, prepare the sauce. Combine all of the ingredients in a blender and blend until smooth.

5. Serve the salmon hot from the oven, drizzled with the tahini lemon sauce.

TIP: This salmon goes perfectly with tabouli, chickpea salad, or boiled new potatoes.

Spicy Fish Tacos

SERVES : 2
PREPARATION TIME : 10 MINUTES
COOKING TIME : 12 MINUTES

You don't have to stand in line at a food truck to get your favorite fish tacos. This homemade version combines spicy cod with a refreshing slaw.

SHOPPING LIST

For the Slaw

- ⅓ head red cabbage, shredded
- ½ large carrot, grated
- ¼ red onion, thinly sliced
- ¼ cup (60 ml) red wine vinegar
- 2 tbsp. water
- ¼ tsp. salt
- ¼ tsp. brown sugar
- ½ tsp. red pepper flakes

For the Fish

- 8 oz. (225 g) thick-cut cod pieces
- 2 tsp. olive oil
- ¼ tsp. red pepper flakes
- ½ tsp. salt
- ½ tsp. ground black pepper
- 4–6 corn tortillas, toasted
- Lime wedges, avocado, and salsa, for serving

NOTES

1. Combine the cabbage, carrot, and onion in a large bowl. Whisk the vinegar, water, salt, sugar, and red pepper flakes together in a separate bowl, then pour over the cabbage mixture and stir. Set aside until your fish is ready. The slaw can be made up to 2 hours ahead of time, if you wish.

2. Preheat a large skillet over medium-high heat. Drizzle the cod with olive oil and season with the red pepper flakes, salt, and pepper. Brown the fish in the skillet for 3 to 6 minutes on each side, or until cooked through.

3. To assemble the tacos, place a few large pieces of the fish into a toasted tortilla. Top with a squeeze of lime, two or three slices of avocado, a little salsa, and 2 tablespoons of the slaw. Serve immediately.

TIP: This easy lime cream will liven up your tacos. Stir together ½ cup (120 ml) sour cream, 2 teaspoons lime juice, and ½ teaspoon lime zest. Spoon on top of the tacos.

Chicken Cordon Bleu Burgers

SERVES : 2
PREPARATION TIME : 10 MINUTES
COOKING TIME : 20 MINUTES

Instead of swinging by the drive-thru for your usual burger and fries, try this unique take on the diner classic the next time you get the burger blues.

SHOPPING LIST

- 12 oz. (340 g) ground chicken
- 1 garlic clove, minced
- 2 tsp. Worcestershire sauce
- ½ tsp. salt
- ¼ tsp. ground black pepper
- 4 thin slices deli ham
- ½ cup (40 g) shredded Swiss cheese
- 1 tbsp. vegetable oil
- 2 tbsp. Dijon mustard
- 2 tbsp. mayonnaise
- 2 brioche buns
- Lettuce, sliced tomato, and sliced onion, to serve

NOTES

1. In a bowl, combine the ground chicken, garlic, Worcestershire sauce, salt, and pepper, taking care not to overmix.

2. Shape the mixture into four even patties, about ½-inch (1.3 cm) thick. Place a slice of ham on the center of two of the patties, divide the Swiss cheese between them, then top with another slice of ham and another patty. Seal the edges of the patties.

3. Heat the oil in a medium skillet over medium-high heat. Sear the burgers for about 6 minutes on each side, flipping once, until the chicken is no longer pink.

4. Stir together the Dijon mustard and mayonnaise.

5. Serve the chicken burgers on the brioche buns topped with the mayo mixture, lettuce, tomato, and onion.

TIPS: It's important that chicken is cooked through, so check the burgers and, if necessary, cook them for longer. If you cannot find ground chicken, ground turkey works just as well.

Chicken Naan Pizza

SERVES : 2
PREPARATION TIME : 10 MINUTES
COOKING TIME : 12 MINUTES

If you don't make pizza at home because you don't have time to make the dough, you'll love this foolproof naan pizza with zesty Southwestern toppings.

SHOPPING LIST

- O 1 boneless, skinless chicken breast, pounded to ½-inch (1.3 cm) thickness and cut into strips
- O ½ tsp. salt
- O ¼ tsp. ground black pepper
- O 1 tbsp. olive oil
- O ¼ cup (60 g) fire-roasted salsa
- O 2 naan flatbreads
- O ½ cup (40 g) shredded Monterey Jack cheese
- O ¼ cup (35 g) frozen corn, thawed
- O ¼ cup (40 g) canned black beans, drained and rinsed
- O ½ poblano pepper, diced
- O 2 tsp. lime juice
- O ½ tsp. lime zest
- O ½ cup (120 ml) sour cream
- O 1 tbsp. finely chopped cilantro leaves
- O ¼ cup (40 g) cherry tomatoes, quartered
- O ½ large avocado, diced

NOTES

....
....
....
....
....

1. Preheat the oven to 400°F (200°C). Season the chicken with the salt and pepper. Heat the olive oil in a medium skillet over medium-high heat. Add the chicken and cook for 3 to 4 minutes or until cooked through, stirring frequently. Set aside.

2. Spoon the fire-roasted salsa evenly over the naan flatbreads and sprinkle with the cheese. Top with the chicken, corn, black beans, and poblano pepper. Place on a sheet pan and bake for 5 to 8 minutes, or until the cheese is completely melted.

3. While the flatbreads are baking, whisk together the lime juice, lime zest, and sour cream.

4. Top the baked flatbreads with the cilantro, tomatoes, and avocado. Drizzle with the lime sour cream and serve the pizzas immediately.

TIP: Now that you see how easy it is to make a naan pizza, you can get creative! Pick your usual favorite delivery toppings and swap out the ones in this recipe.

Skillet Chicken Parmesan

SERVES : 2
PREPARATION TIME : 10 MINUTES
COOKING TIME : 20 MINUTES

There's no need to shell out big bucks at a fancy Italian restaurant for good Chicken Parm. Once you see how easy it is to prepare, you'll make it every week.

SHOPPING LIST

For the Sauce

O One 28-oz. (794 g) can crushed tomatoes

O 2½ tsp. Italian seasoning

O 1 garlic clove, minced

O ½ tsp. salt

O ¼ tsp. ground black pepper

O 1 tsp. sugar

For the Chicken

O ¾ cup (100 g) dried breadcrumbs

O 3 tbsp. grated Parmesan cheese

O 1½ tsp. finely chopped fresh oregano (or ½ tsp. dried oregano)

O ½ cup (70 g) all-purpose flour

O 1 large egg, beaten

O Two 6-ounce (170 g) boneless, skinless chicken breast cutlets, pounded flat

O 1 tbsp. extra virgin olive oil

O 4 oz. (115 g) mozzarella cheese, sliced

O ¼ cup (3 g) fresh basil, to garnish

O Cooked spaghetti, to serve

1. Preheat the oven to 425°F (220°C). In a shallow dish, combine the breadcrumbs, Parmesan, and oregano, tossing together until well combined. Place the flour in another shallow dish and the beaten egg in a third. Dip one of the chicken cutlets in the flour, shaking off the excess. Then dip it into the egg, allowing the excess to run off. Finally, dredge it in the breadcrumbs until evenly coated on both sides and around the edges, then transfer to a clean plate. Repeat with the second cutlet.

2. In a large saucepan, combine the tomatoes, Italian seasoning, garlic, salt, pepper, and sugar, and bring to a boil over high heat. Reduce the heat to medium-low. Cover and simmer, stirring occasionally, for 4 to 5 minutes.

3. Meanwhile, heat the olive oil in a large, ovenproof skillet over medium-high heat. When the oil is hot, cook the breaded chicken cutlets for 3 minutes on each side, or until golden brown and crisp. Once the chicken is crisp, spoon the sauce around and on top of it, then cover with the slices of mozzarella cheese. Bake for 5 minutes, or until the cheese has completely melted.

4. Remove from the oven, garnish with the basil, and serve hot with spaghetti.

TIP: Try turning this recipe into a sandwich! Toast a couple of hoagie rolls or garlic bread in the oven and pile in your finished Chicken Parmesan. Yum!

NOTES

Italian Sausage & Pepper Subs

SERVES : 2
PREPARATION TIME : 10 MINUTES
COOKING TIME : 20 MINUTES

Mamma mia! If you had an Italian grandmother, she would be very proud of this dinner you're about to make.

SHOPPING LIST

- O 1 tbsp. vegetable oil
- O 2 mild Italian sausage links
- O ½ green bell pepper, thinly sliced
- O ½ red bell pepper, thinly sliced
- O 1 yellow onion, thinly sliced
- O 1 garlic clove, minced
- O ½ tbsp. tomato paste
- O 1 cup (200 g) canned diced tomatoes
- O ¼ tsp. salt
- O ¼ tsp. dried oregano
- O ¼ tsp. dried basil
- O ⅛ tsp. ground black pepper
- O ⅛ tsp. red pepper flakes
- O 2 hoagie rolls, toasted

NOTES

....
....
....
....
....
....
....
....
....
....

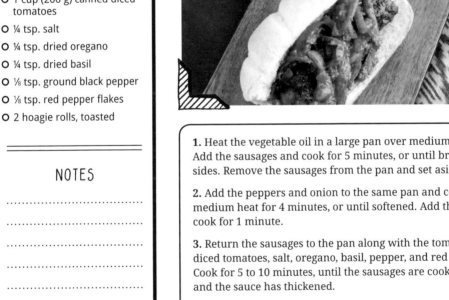

1. Heat the vegetable oil in a large pan over medium-high heat. Add the sausages and cook for 5 minutes, or until browned on all sides. Remove the sausages from the pan and set aside.

2. Add the peppers and onion to the same pan and cook over medium heat for 4 minutes, or until softened. Add the garlic and cook for 1 minute.

3. Return the sausages to the pan along with the tomato paste, diced tomatoes, salt, oregano, basil, pepper, and red pepper flakes. Cook for 5 to 10 minutes, until the sausages are cooked through and the sauce has thickened.

4. Serve on the toasted hoagie rolls.

TIP: Everything's better with cheese, right? To take this sandwich to the next level, top each hoagie with ¼ cup (30 g) of shredded mozzarella cheese. Pop the sandwiches under the broiler for 1 minute to melt the cheese, watching them to make sure they don't burn.

Crispy Herb-Crusted Pork

SERVES : 2
PREPARATION TIME : 10 MINUTES
COOKING TIME : 10 MINUTES

Crisp breadcrumbs and fragrant herbs add a new dimension to these pork cutlets. You can use any herbs, making this a great way to enjoy what you have on hand.

SHOPPING LIST

- 4 thinly sliced pork cutlets
- ½ tsp. salt
- ¼ tsp. ground black pepper
- 1½ cups (210 g) panko breadcrumbs
- 3 tbsp. finely chopped fresh herbs of your choice (such as thyme, rosemary, parsley, tarragon, or oregano) (or 1 tbsp. dried herbs)
- 2 tbsp. grated Parmesan cheese
- ⅔ cup (90 g) all-purpose flour
- 1 egg, lightly beaten
- 2 tbsp. olive oil

NOTES

....
....
....
....
....
....
....
....
....
....
....

1. Season the pork cutlets with the salt and pepper.

2. In a shallow dish, combine the breadcrumbs, herbs, and Parmesan, tossing them together until well combined. Place the flour in another shallow dish and the beaten egg in a third. Preparing the cutlets one at a time, dip one in the flour, shaking off the excess. Follow by dipping it in the egg, allowing the excess to run off. Finally, dredge it in the breadcrumbs until evenly coated on both sides and around the edges, then transfer to a plate while you prepare the remainder of the cutlets.

3. Heat the olive oil in a medium skillet over medium heat. Cook the cutlets for 3 to 5 minutes on each side, until golden brown.

4. Remove the cutlets from the pan. Serve immediately.

TIP: The side dish options for this main course are endless. For the ultimate comfort food dinner, try them with mashed potatoes or macaroni and cheese (page 82).

Swedish Meatballs with Pasta

SERVES : 2
PREPARATION TIME : 10 MINUTES
COOKING TIME : 20 MINUTES

Store-bought meatballs have nothing on the complex flavor of these homemade morsels. The next time you get a hankering for them, try these first.

SHOPPING LIST

- O 8 oz. (225 g) ground beef
- O 2 tbsp. panko breadcrumbs
- O 2 tbsp. finely chopped onion
- O 1½ tsp. finely chopped fresh parsley, plus 1 tbsp. for garnish
- O ⅛ tsp. ground allspice
- O ⅛ tsp. ground nutmeg
- O ¼ tsp. garlic powder
- O Pinch of ground black pepper
- O ¼ tsp. salt
- O 1½ tbsp. beaten egg
- O 2 tsp. sunflower oil
- O 1 cup (100 g) fusilli pasta
- O 2½ tbsp. unsalted butter
- O 1½ tbsp. all-purpose flour
- O 1 cup (240 ml) beef broth
- O ½ cup (120 ml) heavy cream
- O ½ tbsp. Worcestershire sauce
- O ½ tsp. Dijon mustard

NOTES

....
....
....
....
....
....

1. In a bowl, combine the ground beef, breadcrumbs, onion, 1½ teaspoons of parsley, allspice, nutmeg, garlic powder, pepper, salt, and egg. Mix together with your hands to combine.

2. Roll the mixture into 6 to 8 meatballs. Heat the oil in a large skillet over medium-high heat. Add the meatballs and cook, turning, for 8 minutes, until brown all over and cooked through. Transfer to a plate and cover with foil to keep them warm.

3. Cook the pasta according to the package directions.

4. Meanwhile, add the butter and flour to the skillet in which you cooked the meatballs and whisk until there are no lumps. Stir in the broth and cream. Add the Worcestershire sauce and mustard, bring to a simmer, and cook for 10 minutes, stirring all the time, until the sauce starts to thicken.

5. Return the meatballs to the skillet and simmer for 1 to 2 minutes, until piping hot. Serve immediately with the pasta and garnish with the remaining chopped parsley.

Steak with Gorgonzola Sauce

SERVES : 2
PREPARATION TIME : 10 MINUTES
COOKING TIME : 15 MINUTES

Date nights in call for a pretty spectacular meal. Show off your epic culinary skills by whipping up this tender steak with a garlic-Gorgonzola cream sauce.

SHOPPING LIST

- O 2 sirloin steaks, about 1 lb. (450 g) total weight
- O ½ tsp. salt
- O ¼ tsp. ground black pepper
- O ½ tbsp. butter
- O 1 garlic clove, minced
- O ½ tbsp. flour
- O ½ cup (120 ml) heavy cream
- O 3 tbsp. crumbled Gorgonzola cheese, plus 1 tbsp. to garnish

NOTES

....
....
....
....
....
....
....
....
....
....
....
....
....
....
....

1. Season both sides of each steak with the salt and pepper.

2. Heat a medium skillet over high heat and sear the steaks for 2 to 6 minutes on each side, depending on your desired doneness: 2 to 3 minutes each side for rare, 4 minutes each side for medium, and 5 to 6 minutes each side for well done.

3. While the steaks are cooking, melt the butter in a medium saucepan over medium heat. Add the garlic and sauté for 1 minute, until softened. Whisk in the flour, making sure there are no lumps. When the mixture is smooth and thick, add the cream, stirring continuously, until combined. Add the Gorgonzola and whisk until melted and smooth. Set aside.

4. When the steaks are done, transfer them to a plate, cover with a tent of foil, and rest for 2 to 3 minutes before serving. Serve the steaks with the sauce poured on top and garnished with the remaining cheese.

TIP: Add oven fries and a green salad for a French bistro feel.

HOMEMADE TAKEOUT

Instead of getting your grub from a hub, head to the kitchen and whip up a cheaper, healthier, and yes, faster, alternative. These meals can all be made in under 40 minutes.

Chickpea Tikka Masala

SERVES : 2
PREPARATION TIME : 10 MINUTES
COOKING TIME : 20 MINUTES

With flavorful ingredients including fire-roasted tomatoes, coconut, garam masala, and ginger, you won't miss the meat in this hearty vegan curry.

SHOPPING LIST

- O 1 tbsp. canola oil
- O ½ medium onion, diced
- O ½ tsp. salt
- O 1 jalapeño pepper, seeded and finely chopped
- O 2-inch (5 cm) piece ginger, peeled and minced
- O 2 garlic cloves, minced
- O ½ tsp. garam masala
- O ½ tsp. ground cumin
- O ½ tsp. curry powder
- O ¼ tsp. paprika
- O 1½ tbsp. tomato paste
- O 1 cup (200 g) canned fire-roasted tomatoes, diced
- O ½ cup (120 ml) vegetable broth
- O ⅓ cup (80 ml) unsweetened coconut milk
- O 1¼ cups (200 g) canned chickpeas, drained and rinsed
- O 1 tbsp. chopped fresh cilantro
- O Cooked rice (page 113), to serve

1. Heat the oil in a medium pot over medium heat. Add the onion and the salt, and sauté for 3 minutes, until soft, stirring occasionally to keep it from burning. Stir in the jalapeño, ginger, and garlic and cook for an additional 2 minutes. Then add the garam masala, cumin, curry powder, paprika, and tomato paste and cook, stirring, for 2 more minutes.

2. Pour the diced tomatoes with their juices and the vegetable broth into the pot. Bring to a boil and cook for 10 minutes, stirring occasionally. Reduce the heat so that the mixture is simmering. Stir in the coconut milk and chickpeas. Simmer until heated through.

3. Stir in the chopped cilantro and serve immediately over a bed of cooked rice.

TIP: Try topping with a dollop of plain or dairy-free yogurt and scooping with warm naan bread!

NOTES

....

....

....

....

Cashew Chicken

SERVES : 2
PREPARATION TIME : 15 MINUTES
COOKING TIME : 15 MINUTES

The sauce for this stir-fry combines pantry ingredients with chicken and buttery cashew nuts. It's quick to make and bound to become a favorite.

SHOPPING LIST

- ½ cup (65 g) cornstarch
- ¼ tsp. ground black pepper
- ¾ lb. (350 g) boneless, skinless chicken breasts, cut into 1-inch (2.5 cm) pieces
- ½ tbsp. canola oil
- 1 green onion, sliced, to garnish
- Cooked rice (page 113), to serve

For the Sauce
- ¼ cup (60 ml) soy sauce
- 2 tbsp. rice vinegar
- 2 tbsp. ketchup
- 1 tbsp. sweet chili sauce
- 1 tbsp. brown sugar
- 1 clove garlic, minced
- ½ tsp. grated fresh ginger
- ⅛ tsp. red pepper flakes
- ½ cup (70 g) raw cashews

NOTES

....
....
....
....
....
....
....

1. Combine the soy sauce, vinegar, ketchup, chili sauce, sugar, garlic, ginger, pepper flakes, and cashews in a small bowl.

2. Combine the cornstarch and black pepper in a shallow dish. Add the chicken and toss to ensure all of the chicken is coated with the mixture. Shake off the excess.

3. Heat the oil in a large skillet over medium-high heat. Add the chicken and cook for about 2 minutes on each side, until browned.

4. Pour the sauce mixture over the chicken and stir to combine.

5. Simmer the dish for 2 to 3 minutes, or until the sauce has thickened and the chicken is cooked through. Serve immediately over a bed of cooked rice and garnish with the green onions.

TIP: Make sure you get plenty of vitamins by adding a side of steamed bok choy or green beans.

Beef Pho

SERVES : 2
PREPARATION TIME : 15 MINUTES
COOKING TIME : 25 MINUTES

The star of this easy pho is the flavorful broth that's spiced with ginger. Once that's made, all you have to do is add your toppings and get slurping!

SHOPPING LIST

For the Broth

- O 1 onion, halved
- O 3-inch (7.5 cm) piece ginger, peeled
- O 4 cups (960 ml) low-sodium beef broth
- O 2 cups (480 ml) water
- O 2 star anise
- O 2 cloves
- O 1 cinnamon stick
- O 2 tbsp. fish sauce
- O 1 tsp. sugar

For the Toppings

- O 4 oz. (115 g) rice noodles
- O ½ tbsp. canola oil
- O 5½ oz. (155 g) sirloin steak
- O ¼ cup (3 g) fresh cilantro leaves
- O 1 cup (100 g) bean sprouts
- O 6–8 mint leaves
- O 1 lime, sliced into wedges
- O 1 jalapeño pepper, thinly sliced

NOTES

....
....
....
....
....

1. Combine all the ingredients for the broth in a medium-sized pot, and bring to a boil over high heat. Once boiling, stir, lower the heat, and simmer uncovered for 20 minutes.

2. While the broth is simmering, prepare the noodles according to the package directions. Once softened, drain and set aside. Heat the oil in a skillet over high heat and sear the beef for 2 minutes on each side. Cut into ⅛-inch (3 mm) slices.

3. When the broth is cooked, strain into a clean pan and discard the onion, star anise, cloves, ginger, and cinnamon stick.

4. Divide the noodles between two bowls and pour the broth over them. Add the steak, cilantro, bean sprouts, and mint. Garnish with lime wedges and jalapeño slices and serve immediately.

TIP: To make a quick chicken pho, swap out the beef broth for chicken broth and use cooked chicken breast in place of the sirloin steak. There's no need to sear the chicken—just add it to the broth with the rest of the toppings.

Beef with Broccoli and Pineapple

SERVES : 2
PREPARATION TIME : 10 MINUTES
COOKING TIME : 15 MINUTES

Sweet and savory lovers, rejoice! This simple stir-fry takes less than 30 minutes, start to finish, and combines tasty beef and chunks of sweet pineapple.

SHOPPING LIST

- 2 tsp. canola oil
- ½ lb. (225 g) flank steak, sliced into ¼-inch (5 mm) strips
- ¼ cup (60 ml) low-sodium soy sauce
- ½ cup (120 ml) pineapple juice
- ½ tbsp. rice vinegar
- 2 tbsp. brown sugar
- 1½ tsp. cornstarch
- ⅔ cup (100 g) small broccoli florets
- 1 clove garlic, minced
- 2 tbsp. beef broth
- ¼ cup (35 g) pineapple chunks
- ⅛ tsp. salt
- ⅛ tsp. ground black pepper
- Cooked rice (page 113), to serve

NOTES

....
....
....
....
....
....
....
....
....

1. Heat the oil in a large skillet over medium heat. Add the beef and cook until for 3 to 5 minutes, stirring frequently, until browned all over. Transfer to a plate and set aside.

2. Combine the soy sauce, pineapple juice, vinegar, sugar, and cornstarch in a small bowl and whisk until smooth.

3. Add the broccoli and garlic to the pan, and stir. Add the beef broth and simmer for 4 to 6 minutes, or until the broccoli is crisp-tender, stirring occasionally. Return the beef to the pan.

4. Pour the sauce mixture over the beef and broccoli. Add the pineapple chunks, salt, and pepper. Simmer for 1 to 2 minutes, stirring occasionally, until the sauce is thick and bubbly. Serve immediately over a bed of cooked rice.

TIP: You can use fresh or canned pineapple in this dish.

Spicy Sweet Potato Taco Bowls

SERVES : 8
PREPARATION TIME : 15 MINUTES
COOKING TIME : 20 MINUTES

Sure, it's easy to swing by your favorite Mexican restaurant and order a taco bowl to go, but it's healthier and more affordable to make your own.

SHOPPING LIST

- ½ cup (65 g) rice
- ½ tbsp. chili powder
- 1 tsp. sweet smoked paprika
- 1 tsp. ground cumin
- ½ tsp. salt
- 1 tsp. dried oregano
- ¼ tsp. garlic powder
- ¼ tsp. onion powder
- Pinch cayenne pepper
- 1 lb. (450 g) sweet potatoes, peeled and chopped into ½-inch (1.2 cm) cubes
- 1 tbsp. vegetable oil
- 1 cup (175 g) canned black beans, drained and rinsed
- ½ cup (70 g) frozen corn, defrosted
- 1 cup (160 g) cherry tomatoes, halved
- ½ medium avocado, peeled and sliced
- ½ limes, cut into wedges
- 2 tbsp. sour cream
- 1 tbsp. chopped fresh cilantro
- 1 green onion, sliced

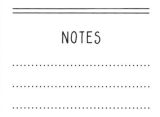

NOTES

....
....
....

1. Preheat the oven to 400°F (200°C). Cook the rice following the instructions on page 113.

2. Meanwhile, in a small bowl, mix together the chili powder, paprika, cumin, salt, oregano, garlic power, onion powder, and cayenne pepper.

3. Place the sweet potato cubes on a baking sheet and toss them with the oil and the seasoning mixture. Bake for 15 to 20 minutes, or until cooked through. When the rice is cooked, drain and set aside until required.

4. To serve, spoon the desired amount of sweet potatoes, rice, black beans, corn, tomatoes, and avocado into a bowl. Garnish with a lime wedge, sour cream, cilantro, and green onions.

TIP: If you're cooking for guests, try serving everything family-style. Place all of the toppings in separate bowls and allow your friends and family to build their bowls how they like. Serve with a variety of hot sauces and tortilla chips for scooping.

COOK NOW, EAT LATER

Get a jump start on your meals for the week by pre-prepping and batch cooking. These recipes will allow you to get ahead so you can enjoy home-cooked food all week.

Veggie Chili with Squash

SERVES : 6–8
PREPARATION TIME : 20 MINUTES
COOKING TIME : 50 MINUTES

You won't believe how hearty this vegetarian chili is. If you make it at the beginning of the week, you'll have a couple of filling lunches and something for the freezer.

SHOPPING LIST

- O 2 tbsp. olive oil
- O 1 medium white onion, diced
- O 1½ lb. (690 g) butternut squash, peeled, seeded, and chopped into ½-inch (1.2 cm) cubes
- O 4 garlic cloves, minced
- O 1 tbsp. chili powder
- O 1 tsp. ground cumin
- O ¼ tsp. ground cinnamon
- O 1 bay leaf
- O One 15-oz. (430 g) can black beans, drained and rinsed
- O One 15-oz. (430 g) can chili beans
- O One 15-oz. (430 g) can pinto beans, drained and rinsed
- O One 14-oz. (400 g) can diced tomatoes
- O 4 cups (1 L) vegetable broth
- O ¾ cup (135 g) quinoa, rinsed
- O 1 tsp. salt
- O ½ tsp. ground black pepper
- O ⅓ cup (15 g) chopped fresh cilantro, to garnish
- O ½ cup (120 ml) sour cream

1. Heat the olive oil in a 4- to 6-quart (4 to 5.7 L) Dutch oven over medium heat. Add the onion and butternut squash and cook, stirring occasionally, for 5 minutes, or until the onions are translucent.

2. Turn the heat down to medium-low and add the garlic, chili powder, cumin, and cinnamon. Cook, stirring constantly, for 30 seconds or until fragrant. Add the bay leaf, beans, tomatoes, broth, and quinoa. Stir to combine and when the mixture starts to simmer, reduce the heat to low, cover and cook for 45 minutes, stirring occasionally, until thick and chunky. Serve topped with the fresh chopped cilantro and a dollop of sour cream.

TIP: This recipe can be adapted for your slow cooker. All you have to do is add all of the ingredients except the cilantro and sour cream to the bowl of your slow cooker and stir to combine. Cook on low for 6 hours, or high for 3 hours.

NOTES

....
....
....
....

Slow Cooker Ramen

SERVES : 8
PREPARATION TIME : 15 MINUTES
COOKING TIME : 8½ HOURS

Making ramen at home might seem like an impossible task. But thanks to your slow cooker, this dish prepares itself and is full of the flavor you know and love.

SHOPPING LIST

- O 3 lb. (1.4 kg) boneless pork shoulder, cut into 3 equal pieces, if needed, to fit in your slow cooker
- O 2 tsp. salt
- O 1 yellow onion, peeled and coarsely chopped
- O 6 garlic cloves, minced
- O 2-inch (5 cm) piece fresh ginger, peeled and chopped
- O 1 leek, halved lengthwise and coarsely chopped (white and green parts)
- O 2 cups (120 g) coarsely chopped cremini mushrooms
- O 8 cups (2 L) chicken broth
- O 2 tbsp. low-sodium soy sauce
- O 2 tsp. sesame oil
- O 1½ lb. (570 g) ramen noodles
- O 8 large eggs, soft-boiled and halved
- O 4 green onions, finely chopped

1. Combine the pork, salt, onion, garlic, ginger, leek, mushrooms, and broth in the bowl of a slow cooker. Cover and cook on low for 8 hours, or until the pork is very tender.

2. Transfer the pork to a cutting board. Using two forks, break the pork into chunks, removing any large pieces of fat. Strain the broth into a bowl and discard the solids. Use a large spoon to remove any fat from the surface of the broth. Return the pork and broth to the slow cooker with the soy sauce and sesame oil. Cover and cook on low for 30 minutes, or until warmed through.

3. For a crowd, cook the noodles according to the package directions. Divide the noodles among eight bowls and ladle the broth and pork over them. Top each bowl with the egg halves and green onions.

4. For two, cook 6 oz. (170g) ramen noodles. Divide the noodles between two bowls, top each with two egg halves and green onions. After dinner, when the broth has cooled completely, fill three freezer bags with the pork and broth. Each bag will contain two servings. Place the sealed bags on a baking sheet so that they freeze flat before storing. Freeze for up to 3 months and defrost before reheating.

TIP: If you like the outside of your pork to be browned, sear it on the stove. Season the pork with salt and heat 2 tablespoons of canola oil in a large skillet over medium-high heat. Sear each side of the pork for 3 to 4 minutes, or until golden brown. Transfer to the slow cooker and continue cooking as directed.

NOTES

Slow Cooker Pulled Pork

SERVES : 8
PREPARATION TIME : 5 MINUTES
COOKING TIME : 12 HOURS

The sky's the limit when it comes to using pulled pork. Whether you're making BBQ sliders or carnitas tacos, this simple recipe is key for quick weeknight meals.

SHOPPING LIST

- O 2 tsp. ground cumin
- O 1 tbsp. garlic powder
- O 1 tbsp. onion powder
- O 1 tbsp. chili powder
- O 1 tsp. cayenne pepper
- O 1 tbsp. salt
- O 2 tsp. ground black pepper
- O 1 tbsp. paprika
- O ¼ cup (50 g) brown sugar
- O 3–6 lb. (1.4 to 2.7 kg) pork shoulder
- O 8–10 dashes Worcestershire sauce

NOTES

....
....
....
....
....
....
....
....
....
....
....
....
....

1. Combine the cumin, garlic powder, onion powder, chili powder, cayenne pepper, salt, pepper, paprika, and brown sugar in a small bowl. Rub the spice mixture all over the pork shoulder.

2. Place the meat in the bowl of your slow cooker and sprinkle the top of the meat with the Worcestershire sauce. Cook on high for 5 to 6 hours. Leave the meat in the slow cooker on the warm setting for another 4 hours, or until it is easy to pull the meat apart with two forks.

3. Remove the meat from the slow cooker and allow to rest for 5 to 10 minutes. Shred the meat, adding any leftover cooking juices, if desired. Store the cooled pork in an airtight container in the fridge for up to three days, or wrap portions in plastic wrap and freezer for up to three months.

TIPS: Try making a Cuban sandwich by layering the pulled pork with ham, Swiss cheese, yellow mustard, and dill pickles on a buttered Cuban loaf or French bread. Or replace the fish in the Spicy Fish Tacos (page 49) with some of the pork.

Easy Chicken Tagine

SERVES : 8
PREPARATION TIME : 35 MINUTES
COOKING TIME : 1¼ HOURS

If you love mixing sweet and savory, you'll adore this tagine. Luscious apricots and honey mellow the spicy kick of cumin and harissa.

SHOPPING LIST

- 2 tsp. salt
- 2 tsp. harissa or chili powder
- 2 tsp. ground cumin
- 2 tsp. ground turmeric
- 2 tsp. ground cinnamon
- 8–12 bone-in, skinless chicken thighs (about 3 lb./1.4 kg)
- 3 cups (720 ml) chicken broth
- 4 tbsp. honey
- 4 tbsp. tomato paste
- 4 tbsp. lemon juice
- 2 tbsp. olive oil
- 2 large onions, halved and thinly sliced lengthwise
- 3 tbsp. minced fresh ginger
- 4 cloves garlic, minced
- 1⅓ cups (215 g) coarsely chopped dried apricots
- 10-oz. (280 g) package couscous, to serve
- 4 tbsp. toasted slivered almonds
- ½ cup (20 g) chopped fresh mint

NOTES

....
....
....
....

1. Combine the salt, harissa, cumin, turmeric, and cinnamon in a bowl. Rub the mixture all over the chicken. Whisk together the broth, honey, tomato paste, and lemon juice in a medium bowl.

2. Heat the olive oil in a skillet over medium heat. Cook half the chicken for 3 minutes on each side, until lightly browned. Remove to a plate. Repeat with the remaining chicken.

3. Reduce the heat to medium, add the onions to the pan, and cook for 10 minutes, stirring occasionally, until they are tender and translucent. Add the ginger and garlic and sauté for another 2 minutes. Return the chicken to the pan.

4. Pour the broth mixture over the chicken. Bring the mixture to a simmer, reduce the heat to low, cover, and cook for 40 to 50 minutes, or until the chicken is tender.

5. Prepare the couscous according to package directions. Serve with the chicken and topped with the almonds and mint. Store the cooled leftover tagine in an airtight container in the fridge for up to three days, or the freezer for up to three months.

Chicken Cacciatore

SERVES : 6
PREPARATION TIME : 15 MINUTES
COOKING TIME : 40 MINUTES

This hunter's stew is a classic of Italian cuisine—and now it will be in your home, too. Serve with rice, pasta, or polenta for a complete feast.

SHOPPING LIST

- 6 bone-in, skinless chicken thighs
- 1 tsp. salt
- ½ tsp. pepper
- 2 tbsp. olive oil
- 1 medium onion, peeled and coarsely chopped
- 8 cloves of garlic, minced
- 1 yellow bell pepper, seeded and diced
- 1 red bell pepper, seeded and diced
- 5 cups (300 g) sliced mushrooms
- 8 to 10 sprigs fresh thyme (or 1 tsp. dried thyme)
- 2 tbsp. chopped fresh parsley
- 2 tbsp. shredded fresh basil
- 1 tsp. finely chopped fresh oregano (or ¼ tsp. dried oregano)
- ⅔ cup (160 ml) red wine
- One 28-oz. (790g) can crushed tomatoes
- 2 tbsp. tomato paste
- ½ tsp. red pepper flakes
- ½ cup (70 g) pitted Kalamata olives
- 7 oz. (200 g) Roma tomatoes, halved
- 3 sprigs fresh rosemary
- 1 sprig fresh basil

1. Season the chicken with the salt and pepper. Heat the oil in a large skillet over medium heat. Add the chicken and sear on both sides until golden. Remove to a plate.

2. Sauté the onion for 3 to 4 minutes, or until transparent. Add the garlic and sauté for 30 seconds, or until fragrant. Add the peppers, mushrooms, thyme, parsley, basil, and oregano and sauté for 5 minutes, or until the vegetables are starting to soften.

3. Return the chicken to the pot. Pour in the wine, scraping any brown bits off the bottom of the skillet. Simmer for 5 to 6 minutes, or until the wine is reduced by half.

4. Stir in the crushed tomatoes, tomato paste, and red pepper flakes. Cover the pan with a lid and reduce the heat to low. Simmer, stirring occasionally, for 30 to 40 minutes or until the chicken is tender. Add the olives and Roma tomatoes and simmer for another 10 minutes, or until warmed through. The finished sauce should be thick enough to coat the chicken. Serve garnished with the remaining parsley, the rosemary, and basil. Store the cooled leftover stew in an airtight container in the fridge for up to three days, or the freezer for up to three months.

NOTES

....
....
....
....
....
....
....
....
....

Boeuf Bourguignon

SERVES : 8
PREPARATION TIME : 30 MINUTES
COOKING TIME : 1¼ HOURS

If it's good enough for Julia Child, it's good enough for you. This version of boeuf bourguignon is considerably simpler than Julia's recipe but is just as delicious.

SHOPPING LIST

- O 1 tbsp. olive oil
- O 8 oz. (230 g) applewood smoked bacon, diced
- O 2½ lb. (1.2 kg) chuck beef cut into 1-inch (2.5 cm) cubes
- O 1 tsp. salt
- O 1 tsp. ground black pepper
- O 1 lb. (450 g) baby carrots
- O 2 yellow onions, peeled, halved, and sliced
- O 2 cloves garlic, minced
- O 1 bottle (750 ml) dry red wine
- O 2 cups (480 ml) beef broth
- O 1 tbsp. tomato paste
- O 2 tsp. fresh thyme leaves (or ¾ tsp. dried)
- O 2 tbsp. unsalted butter, at room temperature
- O 3 tbsp. all-purpose flour
- O 3½ cups (450 g) frozen pearl onions
- O 7½ cups (450 g) thickly sliced mushrooms
- O French bread, to serve

NOTES

....
....
....
....

1. Preheat the oven to 250ºF (120ºC). Heat the olive oil in a large Dutch oven. Add the bacon and cook over medium heat for 10 minutes, stirring occasionally, until golden brown. Use a slotted spoon to remove the bacon to a plate, reserving the drippings.

2. Pat the cubes of beef dry with paper towels and season with the salt and pepper. Working in batches, place a single layer of beef in the pan and sear for 3 to 5 minutes, or until it is brown on all sides. Remove the seared cubes to the plate with the bacon and continue searing the beef until it is all browned. Set aside.

3. Add the carrots and onions to the pan and cook for 10 to 15 minutes, stirring occasionally, until the onions are lightly browned. Add the garlic and cook for 1 minute. Return the beef and bacon to the pan with any juices that have gathered on the plate. Add the wine, broth, tomato paste, and 1 teaspoon thyme. Bring to a simmer, cover the pot with a tight-fitting lid, and bake for 1 hour and 15 minutes, or until the meat and vegetables are tender.

4. Use a fork to combine the butter and flour to make a smooth paste, and stir into the pan. Place the pot on the stove, add the onions and mushrooms, and bring to a boil. Lower the heat and simmer for 15 minutes. Garnish with the remaining thyme, and serve with French bread.

TIP: To make in a slow cooker, begin by cooking bacon in a large skillet over medium-high heat until crisp. Place the bacon in the bowl of the slow cooker. Season the beef with the salt and pepper, add to the skillet in batches and sear on each side for 2 to 3 minutes, until browned on all sides. Transfer the beef to the slow cooker. Add half of the red wine to the skillet, scraping down the brown bits on the side. Simmer for 5 minutes, until reduced slightly, then add the broth and tomato paste. Combine the butter and flour with a fork and stir into the sauce. Transfer the sauce to the slow cooker and add the remaining ingredients. Cook on low for 8 to 10 hours.

ONE-POT WONDERS

Doing the dishes is the worst part of cooking. Here are some one-pot recipes that allow you to make a meal from start to finish in one pan or pot with minimal cleanup.

Moroccan Chicken Skillet

SERVES : 2
PREPARATION TIME : 15 MINUTES
COOKING TIME : 40 MINUTES

When a trip to North Africa isn't on the cards, this flavorful chicken dish is the next best thing! You'll be transported as soon as the lemons hit the pan.

SHOPPING LIST

- ○ ½ small lemon, cut into thin slices, seeds removed
- ○ 1 tbsp. olive oil
- ○ 4 medium chicken thighs
- ○ 1 yellow onion, diced
- ○ 1 garlic clove, minced
- ○ ½ tsp. ground ginger
- ○ ½ tsp. paprika
- ○ ½ tsp. ground cumin
- ○ ½ tsp. turmeric
- ○ ¼ tsp. ground cinnamon
- ○ ½ tsp. salt
- ○ ¼ tsp. ground black pepper
- ○ ½ cup (120 ml) water
- ○ ⅓ cup (45 g) pitted green olives
- ○ 2 tsp. lemon juice, to garnish
- ○ 1 tbsp. finely chopped fresh parsley, to garnish

1. Heat a large skillet over medium-high heat. Add the lemon slices and cook for 1 to 2 minutes on each side, until caramelized. Set aside.

2. Heat the oil in the same pan over medium-high heat. Add the chicken, skin side down. Cook for 3 to 5 minutes on each side, until browned. Remove to a plate.

3. Add the onion to the oil in the pan, reduce the heat to low, and cook until soft and translucent, 5 to 7 minutes. Add the garlic, all the spices, and the salt and pepper. Stir for 1 minute, scraping up the brown bits on the bottom of the pan. Stir in the water.

4. Return the chicken to the pan. Bring the mixture to a simmer, reduce the heat, cover, and simmer for 15 minutes.

5. Stir in the olives and lemon juice. Garnish with the charred lemon slices and fresh parsley and serve immediately.

TIP: This dish pairs well with couscous.

NOTES

....
....
....
....

Chicken, Kale & Orzo Soup

SERVES : 2
PREPARATION TIME : 10 MINUTES
COOKING TIME : 20 MINUTES

This definitely isn't your mother's chicken noodle soup. With superfoods like kale, turmeric, and lemon, this recipe is a modern take on a classic dish.

SHOPPING LIST

- O 1 tsp. olive oil
- O ⅓ medium yellow onion, chopped
- O ½ tsp. salt
- O ¼ tsp. ground black pepper
- O 2 garlic cloves, minced
- O 2⅓ cups (560 ml) chicken broth
- O ½ tsp. dried oregano
- O 1 tsp. ground turmeric
- O 1 cup (150 g) cooked and shredded chicken breast
- O ⅓ cup (40 g) dried orzo pasta
- O 1⅔ cups (25 g) roughly chopped kale
- O ½ tsp. lemon zest
- O 2 tbsp. lemon juice

NOTES

....
....
....
....
....
....
....
....
....
....

1. Heat the olive oil in a large pot over medium-high heat. Add the onion, salt, and pepper and sauté for 3 minutes. Add the garlic and sauté for another minute, until it is fragrant.

2. Add the chicken broth, oregano, turmeric, and chicken to the pot. Bring to a simmer.

3. Add the orzo to the pot, reduce the heat to medium-low, and cover. Simmer, stirring occasionally, for 6 minutes. Add the kale and cook for another 2 to 4 minutes, or until the orzo is al dente.

4. Stir in the lemon zest and juice and simmer until the orzo is cooked to your liking. Serve warm.

TIPS: If you decide to make this soup ahead of time, or have leftovers, you may need to add a bit of water or chicken stock when reheating, as the pasta will absorb some of the liquid as the soup cools. To make the soup with raw chicken, cut 1 cup (150 g) chicken breast into small pieces and add to the pot with the broth.

Coconut-Braised Chicken Thighs

SERVES : 2
PREPARATION TIME : 5 MINUTES
COOKING TIME : 50 MINUTES

Sweet meets savory in this healthy, tropical-inspired chicken feast. Trust me, you're going to go coco-nuts for this one.

SHOPPING LIST

- 1 tbsp. coconut oil
- 8 oz. (225 g) boneless, skinless chicken thighs
- ½ tsp. salt
- ¼ tsp. ground black pepper
- 1 large sweet potato, peeled and cut into large chunks
- One 13½-oz. (383 g) can light coconut milk
- 2 cups (240 g) roughly chopped kale
- 2 cups (240 g) cooked quinoa (½ cup/90 g uncooked)
- ¼ cup (20 g) unsweetened coconut flakes, to garnish

NOTES

....
....
....
....
....
....
....
....
....
....
....
....

1. Heat the coconut oil in a large skillet over medium-high heat. Season the chicken thighs with the salt and pepper and cook for about 4 minutes on each side, until browned.

2. Remove the chicken from the skillet and add the sweet potato. Sauté until slightly browned, about 5 minutes.

3. Return the chicken to the skillet with the sweet potatoe and add the coconut milk. Cover and simmer for 20 minutes, until the potatoes are almost tender.

4. Uncover the skillet, increase the heat to medium-high, and bring to a boil. Cook for 5 minutes, or until the sauce is thickened and reduced. Add the kale and cook for 5 minutes more, or until the leaves are wilted and tender. Serve immediately with quinoa and topped with the coconut flakes.

TIP: Be sure you don't get canned coconut milk confused with the kind in the carton. You want a nice thick sauce, so canned is preferred.

Chicken Cordon Bleu Hot Dish

SERVES : 2
PREPARATION TIME : 20 MINUTES
COOKING TIME : 30 MINUTES

If you're scratching your head at the name of this dish, you're probably not alone. Hot dish is a casserole with a topping of crispy potato puffs. You're welcome.

SHOPPING LIST

- 1 tbsp. unsalted butter
- ⅓ onion, chopped
- 1 garlic clove, minced
- 1 oz. (30 g) diced ham
- 1 tbsp. flour
- 1½ cups (120 ml) whole milk
- ¾ cup (60 g) shredded Swiss cheese
- 1 cup (125 g) cooked, shredded chicken
- ⅓ cup (40 g) frozen peas
- ½ tsp. salt
- ¼ tsp. ground black pepper
- 30–40 potato puffs, from a 32-oz. (907 g) bag
- 2 slices thick-cut bacon, pan-fried and crumbled, to serve
- 1 tbsp. finely chopped parsley, to garnish

1. Preheat the oven to 350°F (175°C). Melt the butter in a medium ovenproof skillet over medium-high heat. Add the onion, garlic, and ham. Sauté until the onions are soft, about 5 minutes.

2. Sprinkle the flour over the mixture and stir to coat. When you can't see any more dry flour, add the milk slowly, stirring after each addition, until smooth. Add the shredded Swiss cheese and stir until melted.

3. Stir in the chicken and peas and season with the salt and pepper. Take off the heat.

4. Top the mixture with a single layer of potato puffs.

5. Bake for 20 to 30 minutes, until the topping is brown and crispy. Let stand for a few minutes before serving topped with the crumbled bacon and garnished with the chopped parsley.

TIPS: If you happen to be out of potato puffs but you have a bag of frozen shredded hash browns in the freezer, those would work as a fine substitute for the topping. If you have more ham than you need, chop it into small pieces and sprinkle it over the hot dish in place of the bacon.

NOTES

Jambalaya

SERVES : 2
PREPARATION TIME : 20 MINUTES
COOKING TIME : 20 MINUTES

Bring the Louisiana bayou into your kitchen with this speedy version of classic jambalaya. If you like your food spicy, this one's for you!

SHOPPING LIST

- ½ cup (125 g) rice
- 2 tbsp. olive oil
- 1 stalk celery, chopped
- ½ white onion, diced
- 1 small red bell pepper, seeded and chopped
- 1 small jalapeño pepper, seeded and finely chopped
- 4 garlic cloves, minced
- 1 boneless, skinless chicken breast, cut into bite-sized pieces
- 4 oz. (115 g) andouille sausage, thinly sliced into rounds
- 4 oz. (115 g) raw shrimp, peeled and deveined
- ¼ cup (25 g) thinly sliced okra
- 1 cup (240 g) crushed tomatoes
- 1 tbsp. Cajun seasoning
- 1 bay leaf
- ½ tsp. dried thyme
- ½ tsp. salt
- ¼ tsp. ground black pepper
- 1 tbsp. finely chopped fresh parsley

1. Cook the rice following the instructions on page 113.

2. Meanwhile, heat 1 tablespoon of the oil in a deep skillet over medium-high heat. Add the celery, onion, peppers, jalapeño, and garlic. Sauté for 5 minutes, stirring occasionally, until the vegetables are soft.

3. Add the remaining 1 tablespoon of oil and the chicken and sausage, and stir to combine. Sauté for another 5 minutes, or until the chicken is no longer pink.

4. Drain the rice and stir into the pan with the shrimp, okra, tomatoes, Cajun seasoning, bay leaf, and thyme. Reduce the heat to medium-low, cover, and simmer for 5 more minutes, stirring occasionally, until the shrimp are cooked.

5. Remove the bay leaf. Season the jambalaya with the salt and pepper, sprinkle with the parsley, and serve immediately.

TIP: If you don't like a lot of heat, omit the jalapeño and reduce the Cajun seasoning to 2 teaspoons.

Greek Meatballs with Dill Rice

SERVES : 2
PREPARATION TIME : 10 MINUTES
COOKING TIME : 15 MINUTES

If you thought you made spaghetti and meatballs a lot, wait until you start cooking this recipe. It might just take over as your new favorite meatball dinner.

SHOPPING LIST

- ½ cup (125 g) rice
- 8 oz. (225 g) ground beef
- 2 tbsp. dried breadcrumbs
- ½ tsp. dried oregano
- ¼ tsp. lemon zest
- 1 garlic clove, minced
- 1½ tbsp. beaten egg
- ½ tsp. salt
- ⅛ tsp. ground black pepper
- 2 tsp. olive oil
- 1 zucchini, quartered lengthwise and cut into ¼-inch (5 mm) slices
- 2 tsp. lemon juice
- 2 tbsp. finely chopped fresh dill (or 1 tsp. dried dill)
- 9 cherry tomatoes, halved

NOTES

....
....
....
....
....
....
....
....
....
....

1. Cook the rice following the instructions on page 113.

2. Meanwhile, combine the ground beef, breadcrumbs, oregano, lemon zest, garlic, egg, salt, and pepper in a bowl. Mix with your hands until thoroughly combined. Roll into 6 to 8 meatballs.

3. Heat the olive oil in a large skillet over high heat. Place the meatballs in the pan and cook for 3 to 4 minutes on each side, or until browned all over.

4. Add the zucchini to the pan and sauté for 5 minutes, or until cooked through. Drain the rice and add to the pan with the lemon juice and dill. Stir and continue cooking until the rice is heated through. Place the cherry tomatoes on top. Serve immediately.

TIP: The more sides, the better in my opinion. Try serving this with a dollop of hummus or tzatziki sauce and a few wedges of warm pita.

Creamy No-Bake Mac 'n' Cheese

SERVES : 2
PREPARATION TIME : 10 MINUTES
COOKING TIME : 15 MINUTES

You certainly don't have to be a child to enjoy a big bowl of creamy mac 'n' cheese for dinner! Serve it simply as it is, or dress it up to suit the occasion.

SHOPPING LIST

- 1 cup (240 ml) whole milk
- ¾ cup (180 ml) water
- 1 cup (115 g) small elbow macaroni
- ¼ tsp. salt
- ⅛ tsp. fresh ground black pepper
- ½ cup (40 g) extra-sharp grated Cheddar cheese
- ¼ tsp. garlic powder

NOTES

....
....
....
....
....
....
....
....
....
....
....
....
....
....
....

1. Combine the milk, water, macaroni, salt, and pepper in a medium pot over medium heat. Bring the mixture to a low simmer, stirring frequently. Once it has started to simmer, reduce the heat to medium-low and stir continuously until the pasta is done to your liking, about 8 to 10 minutes. The macaroni will absorb the liquid while cooking, so you may need to stir in additional water 1 tablespoon at a time, as needed.

2. Once the pasta is cooked and the sauce is creamy, remove the pot from the heat and gradually add the grated Cheddar, stirring until it is smooth and melted. Stir in the garlic powder. Serve immediately.

TIP: If you prefer baked macaroni and cheese, make the recipe as instructed. Grease a small baking pan with nonstick cooking spray. Pour the cooked macaroni and cheese into the prepared pan and spread evenly. Cover with foil and refrigerate until you're ready to bake. Preheat the oven to 325ºF (160ºC). Melt 1 tablespoon of unsalted butter in the microwave and stir in ¼ cup (35 g) panko breadcrumbs. Spread the breadcrumb mixture over the top of the macaroni and cheese and bake for 10 to 12 minutes, or until golden brown and bubbly.

Parmesan & Kale Mac 'n' Cheese
Substitute 1 cup (30 g) grated Parmesan cheese for the extra-sharp Cheddar cheese. At the end of step 2, stir in 7 cups (105 g) baby kale. Cook for 2 to 3 minutes, until the kale is wilted.

Broccoli & Ham Mac 'n' Cheese
At the end of step 2, stir in 1 cup (175 g) defrosted frozen broccoli florets and ⅔ cup (100 g) cubed cooked ham. Cook for 2 to 3 minutes, or until they are warmed through.

Spinach & Artichoke Mac 'n' Cheese
Substitute ⅔ cup (50 g) Fontina cheese for the extra-sharp Cheddar cheese. At the end of step 2, stir in 5¾ cups (115 g) fresh spinach and one 14-ounce (400 g) can of drained artichoke quarters. Cook for 2 to 3 minutes, or until the spinach is wilted and the artichokes are warmed through.

Black Bean Enchilada Quinoa

SERVES : 2
PREPARATION TIME : 5 MINUTES
COOKING TIME : 20 MINUTES

Just when you think you've exhausted all of the tasty ways to cook quinoa, this recipe comes along and blows them all out of the water.

SHOPPING LIST

- ½ cup (90 g) quinoa, rinsed
- ½ cup (80 g) canned black beans, rinsed and drained
- ½ large sweet potato, peeled and cut into ¼-inch (5 mm) pieces
- 1 cup (140 g) frozen corn
- ½ cup (100 g) canned diced tomatoes
- 1 tbsp. taco seasoning
- ¼ cup (60 ml) red enchilada sauce
- ¼ cup (60 ml) water
- 1 cup (15 g) chopped kale
- ¼ cup (20 g) grated Monterey Jack cheese
- ½ large avocado, peeled, pitted, and diced
- 2 tbsp. chopped green onions

NOTES

....
....
....
....
....
....
....
....
....

1. In a large skillet, combine the quinoa, black beans, sweet potato, corn, tomatoes, taco seasoning, enchilada sauce, and water. Bring to a boil, cover, reduce the heat and simmer until the quinoa is done, about 15 to 20 minutes, stirring occasionally. If the mixture becomes too dry, add more water, 1 tablespoon at a time, as needed.

2. Stir in the kale and cheese. Serve immediately, topped with the avocado and green onions.

TIP: If you have leftover tortillas, this is a great opportunity to use them. Instead of enjoying the quinoa from a bowl, spoon it into the tortillas for a fun vegetarian taco Tuesday.

Easy Vegetarian Paella

SERVES : 2
PREPARATION TIME : 10 MINUTES
COOKING TIME : 20 MINUTES

You won't notice that this version of the traditional Spanish dish is meat-free, thanks to the fresh veggies and spices.

SHOPPING LIST

- ½ cup (125 g) rice
- 2 tbsp. olive oil
- ½ cup (125 g) tofu, cut into cubes
- ½ onion, chopped
- 2 garlic cloves, minced
- ½ red bell pepper, diced
- ½ medium zucchini, halved lengthwise and sliced
- ¼ cup (60 ml) white wine
- ½ tsp. salt
- ½ tsp. ground black pepper
- ½ tsp. smoked paprika
- ¼ tsp. turmeric
- ¼ cup (35 g) pitted green olives
- ½ cup (90 g) canned artichoke hearts, drained and roughly chopped
- ¼ tsp. pepper flakes
- 1 tbsp. finely chopped fresh parsley
- 2 lemon wedges, to garnish

NOTES

....
....
....
....
....

1. Cook the rice following the instructions on page 113.

2. Meanwhile, heat 1 tablespoon of the olive oil in a large skillet over medium heat. Sauté the tofu cubes for 6 to 8 minutes, until brown and crispy all over. Set aside. Drain the rice.

3. Heat the remaining 1 tablespoon olive oil in the same pan and sauté the onion and the garlic for 2 to 3 minutes. Add the pepper and zucchini and cook for another 3 minutes, until they start to soften. Stir in the rice and cook for another 2 to 3 minutes.

4. Add the white wine to the pan and scrape up any bits that may be stuck to the bottom of the pan. Season with the salt, pepper, paprika, and turmeric.

5. Stir in the olives, tofu, and artichokes. Cook for 2 minutes, or until heated through. Sprinkle with the red pepper flakes and parsley, and serve garnished with the lemon wedges.

TIP: If you can find smoked tofu in your grocery store, it adds a wonderful flavor to this dish.

FOOD WITH FRIENDS

Planning a dinner party doesn't have to be stressful. The main course options in this chapter will guarantee you can host a meal that you'll enjoy as much as your guests do.

Making Dinners to Impress

First of all, check if any of your guests have any food allergies or dietary restrictions, or things they plain don't like. If the dinner is close to the birthday, anniversary, or promotion of one of the guests, plan a special dish that you know they would love. Use the Dinner Party Planner template (page 152) for your lists.

Next consider yourself. Are you a nervous cook? If so, things you can make in advance and take from oven to table fit the bill. If you love drama and can laugh and reach for the pizza menu if your soufflé falls, go wild! For folks who fall between those two extremes, don't overdo it with the new dishes and stick to familiar recipes. Finally, keep an eye on the seasons: in the summer, serve something light and refreshing, while in the winter, stews and roasts are more appropriate.

Decide on your main course and build around that. With a main dish in mind, you can then look at the starter, sides, and dessert and create a balance of complementary flavors. For example, if you're having a hearty stew for the main course, you'd want a light dessert.

For the simplest supper of all, serve an appetizer board that tastes as good as it looks. When the nibbles are this yummy, who needs a main course? Or go the more traditional route and follow a soup (like the Roasted Tomato-Basil Soup on page 105) with a standout vegetarian main course such as the Caprese Stuffed Mushrooms (page 90) or Easy Vegetarian Paella (page 85). For meat eaters, try the Boeuf Bourguignon (page 72) or Roast Citrus Chicken (page 92).

To save your sanity, don't wait until the last minute do all the chopping. Early that morning or even the day before, knock out all of your vegetable washing and dicing and marinating of meat or fish. This restaurant trick will save you so much time in the hours leading up to dinner that you'll be as cool as that cucumber you sliced the day prior.

When it comes to dessert, let your favorite bakery do the work! You're putting in all of the effort on the rest of the meal; the last thing you need is to have to babysit a cake at the same time. Set your pride aside and delegate the perfect end to a foolproof dinner party to the pros.

PARTY TIPS

- Do you want to set a theme? Decide if this is a sophisticated soirée or a relaxed get-together.

- If you want to treat your friends to a new dish, practice it first!

- Flowers and candles make a room look romantic and pretty.

- Make sure there's space in the fridge for the chilled food and drinks.

- And remember that people come for the company, not the food.

PARTY CHECKLIST

2–4 WEEKS BEFORE

- ○ Set a day and time.
- ○ Invite your guests, asking if they have food allergies, special diets, or foods they really hate.
- ○ Plan the menu.
- ○ Create a shopping list.
- ○ Create a playlist.

I WEEK BEFORE

- ○ Plan out the day-of-cooking schedule.
- ○ Pick up any new tools you may need.
- ○ Make sure you have napkins, candles, and other decorations.
- ○ Clean and tidy the rooms your guests will see.
- ○ Plan where everyone will sit.
- ○ Work out where you are going to store guests' coats and bags.

I DAY BEFORE

- ○ Go shopping for groceries.
- ○ Buy dessert.
- ○ Buy fresh flowers.
- ○ Prep ingredients (wash, dice, marinate, etc.).
- ○ Stock the freezer with ice for the drinks.

ON THE DAY

- ○ Do any last-minute cleaning and tidying.
- ○ Remove any personal items from the bathroom cabinet you don't want your friends to see.
- ○ Double-check your schedule.
- ○ Chill the drinks.
- ○ Tidy the kitchen so you have space to work and stack dirty dishes as the evening progresses.
- ○ Begin cooking.
- ○ Set the table.
- ○ Change into your party clothes.
- ○ Plate the dishes.
- ○ Relax and enjoy!

Cheese & Charcuterie Board

SERVES : 6
PREPARATION TIME : 10 MINUTES

I like a board to look generous with three to five cheeses, about 2 to 3 ounces (55 to 85 grams) per person, at least 4 slices of charcuterie each, plus crackers and olives.

SHOPPING LIST

- 9-oz. (255 g) whole Brie
- 4 oz. (115 g) white Cheddar cheese
- 4 oz. (115 g) Colby-Jack cheese
- 12–18 slices prosciutto
- 12–18 slices salami
- 2 cups (320 g) red grapes
- 1 cup (160 g) dried apricots
- 1 cup (140 g) Kalamata olives
- 1 cup (140 g) roasted cashews
- 2 oranges, peeled and divided into segments
- Fresh herbs, to garnish
- Crackers, to serve

NOTES

....
....
....
....
....
....
....
....
....
....
....

1. Arrange the cheeses, meats, fruits, nuts, and crackers on a platter and garnish with herbs.

TIPS: You can add herb-rolled goat cheese, blue cheese, almonds, breadsticks, and roasted red bell peppers to your selection, if desired. If you have any leftover cheese, hard cheeses such as Cheddar and Colby-Jack can be shredded and frozen. Or use them to make Mac 'n' Cheese (page 82).

Vegan Charcuterie Board

SERVES : 6
PREPARATION TIME : 10 MINUTES

Crafting the perfect vegan board isn't very different than preparing its classic counterpart. If you choose vegan cheeses and spreads, you can almost follow the same rules.

SHOPPING LIST

- 12 oz. (340 g) hummus
- 2 cups (320 g) red grapes
- 8 oz. (230 g) baby carrots
- 1 cup (180 g) dried apricots
- 3 oz. (85 g) snow peas
- 1 cup (175 g) broccoli florets
- 1 cup (140 g) Kalamata olives
- 1 cup (140 g) roasted cashews
- 1 apple, sliced
- ½ cup (120 ml) vegan ranch dressing
- Fresh herbs, to garnish
- Crackers, to serve

NOTES

1. Arrange the hummus, fruits, nuts, and crackers on a platter and garnish with herbs. Pour the dressing into a small pitcher.

TIP: You can also add mushroom pâté, a cashew cheese ball, vegan cheese, sliced bell peppers, and celery stalks to your selection.

Caprese Stuffed Mushrooms

SERVES : 2
PREPARATION TIME : 10 MINUTES
COOKING TIME : 7 MINUTES

If you have vegetarians coming to dinner, these stuffed mushrooms are hearty and delicious. Even the meat eaters will be reaching for a serving.

SHOPPING LIST

- O 2 tbsp. unsalted butter
- O 2 cloves garlic, smashed
- O 1 tbsp. fresh parsley, chopped
- O 4 large portobello mushrooms, stems removed
- O 1½ cups (120 g) shredded mozzarella
- O 1 cup (160 g) cherry tomatoes, halved
- O ½ cup (10 g) shredded fresh basil
- O ½ tsp. salt
- O ¼ tsp. ground black pepper
- O Crusty bread and a side salad, to serve

1. Position the oven shelf in the middle of your oven. Turn on the broiler to high, or preheat the oven as high as it will go.

2. Combine the butter, garlic, and parsley in a small saucepan, and cook until the butter has melted and the garlic is fragrant. Brush the tops and bottoms of each mushroom with the garlic butter and place on a baking sheet.

3. Fill each mushroom with ¼ cup (20 g) of the shredded mozzarella and several tomato halves. Place the baking sheet under the broiler, and broil the mushrooms for 3 to 5 minutes, or until the cheese is melted and golden. Be sure to keep an eye on them as they can easily burn under the broiler.

4. Top with the shredded basil and season with the salt and pepper. Serve immediately with crusty bread and a side salad.

TIP: Try serving these stuffed mushrooms with a drizzle of balsamic glaze. To make your own, combine ¼ cup (60 ml) balsamic vinegar with 2 teaspoons of brown sugar in a small saucepan. Bring to a simmer and cook for 5 to 8 minutes, until thick and syrupy.

NOTES

Roasted Citrus Chicken

SERVES : 6–8
PREPARATION TIME : 15 MINUTES
COOKING TIME : 1¾ HOURS

This citrusy recipe ensures your roasted chicken stays juicy and has a ton of bright flavor. It's served with crisp green beans and creamy polenta.

SHOPPING LIST

- One 5–6 lb. (2.3–2.7 kg) whole roasting chicken, patted dry and anything inside the cavity removed
- 1 orange, quartered
- 1 lemon, quartered
- 1 lime, quartered
- 1 head garlic, halved crosswise
- 1 tsp. salt
- ½ tsp. ground black pepper
- ¼ cup (60 ml) freshly squeezed orange juice
- ¼ cup (60 ml) lemon juice
- 2 tbsp. olive oil
- 1 tbsp. chopped fresh rosemary (or ¼ tsp. dried rosemary)

For the Green Beans
- 1 lb. (454 g) fresh green beans, ends trimmed
- 4 tbsp. unsalted butter
- 1 tsp. lemon zest
- ½ tsp. salt
- ¼ tsp. pepper

For the Polenta
- 4 cups (960 ml) chicken broth
- 1 cup (140 g) instant polenta
- ½ cup (15 g) grated Parmesan cheese
- 1 tbsp. unsalted butter

1. Preheat the oven to 400°F (200°C). Stuff the cavity of the chicken with the orange, lemon, lime, and garlic. Using kitchen string, tie the chicken legs together. Season the chicken with salt and pepper.

2. Place the chicken on a rack in a roasting pan. Roast for 1 hour, basting occasionally. Whisk together the orange juice, lemon juice, oil, and rosemary in a medium bowl. Brush some of the juice mixture over the chicken, and roast for another 45 minutes, basting occasionally with the remaining juice mixture. The chicken is cooked when the juices run clear when you cut into the meat and no pink remains. Transfer the chicken to a platter and cover with a tent of aluminum foil until ready to serve.

3. While the chicken roasts, prepare the green beans. Fill a sauté pan with a half-inch (1.2 cm) of water and bring to a boil. Add the beans, cover, and cook for 3 to 5 minutes, or until they are tender but still toothsome.

4. While the chicken rests, prepare the polenta. Bring the broth to a boil in a large pot. Reduce the heat to medium low, and stir in the polenta. Cover, stirring constantly, for 3 minutes, until the polenta thickens. Remove from the heat and stir in the Parmesan and butter.

5. To reheat the beans, melt the butter in a medium nonstick pan over medium heat. Add the lemon zest and continue to cook for 1 minute. Toss the green beans with the lemon butter, salt, and pepper and heat through. Remove from the heat. Serve immediately with the polenta and roast chicken.

TIPS: This versatile roast chicken goes with so many sides! If you have potatoes on hand, prepare your favorite mashed potatoes (page xxx) instead of the polenta. You could also easily swap asparagus or broccoli for the green beans. Don't be put off roasting a chicken if there are just two of you—there will be plenty of leftovers for you to enjoy later in the week. For example, try the Chicken, Kale & Orzo Soup on page 76, or the Greek Chicken Salad Pitas on page 111.

Brown Butter Pork Chops

SERVES : 4
PREPARATION TIME : 10 MINUTES
COOKING TIME : 30 MINUTES

Pork chops are a delicious and elegant alternative to poultry. Try serving them with nutty browned butter and mushrooms.

SHOPPING LIST

- 4 tbsp. olive oil
- 4 bone-in pork chops
- 3 garlic cloves, minced
- Leaves from 4 thyme sprigs (or ¼ tsp. dried thyme)
- 6 tbsp. unsalted butter
- 3¾ cups (225 g) small mushrooms, sliced
- 1 tbsp. chopped fresh parsley
- Mashed potatoes and carrots, to serve

1. Preheat the oven to 450°F (230°C). Heat the oil in a large ovenproof skillet over medium-high heat. Cook the pork chops for 3 to 4 minutes on each side, or until golden brown. Transfer the skillet to the oven and roast the pork chops for 6 minutes.

2. Return the skillet with the chops to the stove over medium heat. Add the garlic, thyme, and butter to the skillet, and cook until the butter is lightly browned and foamy. Use a large spoon to baste the chops with the butter for 2 to 3 minutes until they are firm and the juices run clear when you cut into them. Transfer the pork chops to a serving dish and let them rest.

3. Add the mushrooms to the browned butter and sauté for 5 to 6 minutes, until they are browned and soft. Serve the pork chops with the mushrooms and browned butter poured over the top and sprinkled with parsley.

TIP: Browned butter is one of the easiest flavors you can add to a dish. The key is to take it off of the heat when it starts to smell sweet and nutty and is lightly browned. If you cook it for too long, you'll end up with burned butter and that's not what you're looking for. Serve the pork chops with mashed potatoes (page 113) and carrots.

NOTES

4

THE ZERO-WASTE KITCHEN

There's nothing worse than opening the crisper to find soggy herbs, lifeless veggies, and moldy fruit. To stop wasting precious time and money on ruined produce, take a weekly survey of the contents of your fridge. Throw out anything that's past its sell-by date, freeze anything you know you won't be able to cook during the week, and use the rest to whip up a healthy recipe (or two) for the week ahead.

This chapter will show you how to use leftover ingredients with three versatile recipes: a hearty soup, a zesty stir-fry, and a comforting quiche. Quiches are a great way to use up those last few eggs along with that handful of cheese and leftover meat, while soups and stir-fries are perfect for cooking random vegetables while they're still in their prime. The last section of the chapter will help you solve the problem of ingredient overload, suggesting recipes that'll use up the remainder of that bag of carrots or potatoes, or the other half of a cabbage or cucumber. Upcycle your leftovers to create tasty meals and you'll save money, time, and even help preserve the planet, one recipe at a time!

Super Soup

SERVES : 2
PREPARATION TIME : 10 MINUTES
COOKING TIME : 25 MINUTES

The night before my weekly shopping trip, I make this soup. It's always different and always delicious. This is just one example, made using what I had one week.

SHOPPING LIST

- 1 tbsp. olive oil
- ⅓ onion, diced
- 1 clove garlic, minced
- 1 stalk celery, chopped
- 1 small carrot, sliced
- ½ cup (150 g) small cauliflower florets
- ¼ cup (20 g) shredded red cabbage
- ½ cup (50 g) dried pasta
- 8-oz. (225 g) can diced tomatoes
- 1⅓ cups (320 ml) vegetable broth
- ¼ tsp. Italian seasoning
- ½ tsp. salt
- ¼ tsp. ground black pepper
- ⅓ cup (5 g) shredded kale

1. Heat the oil in a large pot over medium-high heat. Add the onion and garlic and sauté for 2 minutes, stirring occasionally, until softened but not browned.

2. Stir in the celery, carrot, cauliflower, red cabbage, and pasta. Add the tomatoes and vegetable broth and bring to a boil. Reduce the heat and simmer for 10 to 15 minutes, or until the vegetables are crisp-tender.

3. Stir in the Italian seasoning, salt and pepper, and the kale. Simmer for an additional 2 to 3 minutes, or until the kale has started to wilt but still has some texture and the pasta is cooked. Serve immediately.

TIP: For a heartier soup, add cooked chicken, slices of sausage, cubed tofu, canned (or precooked) beans, or lentils along with the pasta.

Soup Inspiration

You can use almost any combination of vegetables for this soup, but be sure to include aromatics such as garlic and onion, vegetables, and some carbs in the form of diced potatoes, pasta, or rice.

TIP: Avoid veggies such as beets which will color a mixed-vegetable soup, and parsnips, which have a very dominant flavor. If you have beets, celebrate them with a bowl of beet soup; show off parsnips with a curried soup.

1. Heat the oil, add the aromatics, and sauté for 2 minutes, until softened but not browned.

AROMATICS:
- Onions, chopped
- Shallots, minced
- Green onions, sliced
- Leeks, diced
- Celery, diced
- Garlic, minced
- Fennel, diced

2. Add the liquid (e.g. broth, water), hard vegetables, and uncooked pasta or rice. Simmer for 10 to 15 minutes, until the veggies are crisp-tender.

THE HARD STUFF:
- Beans, cut into 1-inch (2.5 cm) pieces
- Carrots, cut into ¼-inch (5 mm) rounds
- Potatoes, cut into 1-inch (2.5 cm) cubes
- Summer squash and zucchini, cut into 1-inch (2.5 cm) cubes
- Acorn and butternut squash, cut into 1-inch (2.5 cm) cubes
- Sweet potatoes, cut into 1-inch (2.5 cm) cubes
- Cabbage, shredded

3. Add seasoning and quick-cook or precooked veggies. Simmer for 2 to 3 minutes, until the veggies have wilted and are warmed.

QUICK COOKERS:
- Asparagus, cut into ½-inch (1.3 cm) pieces
- Spinach, shredded
- Kale, shredded
- Greens, shredded
- Mushrooms, sliced
- Pea pods or snow peas
- Canned or frozen garden peas
- Canned or frozen corn
- Cooked rice or pasta

Simple Stir-Fry

SERVES : 2
PREPARATION TIME : 15 MINUTES
COOKING TIME : 25 MINUTES

Stir-fries are a great way to use up excess veggies. Try different combinations of your favorites to create a dinner you'll make again and again.

SHOPPING LIST

- O 3 tbsp. canola oil
- O 1 onion, thinly sliced
- O 4 cloves garlic, minced
- O ¾ tsp. salt, or to taste
- O 1¼ cups (225g) broccoli florets
- O 1 cup (60 g) sliced baby mushrooms
- O ½ red bell pepper, sliced
- O ½ small yellow squash, cut in half lengthwise and thinly sliced
- O 4 oz. (115 g) snow peas
- O ¼ cup (60 ml) rice vinegar
- O 2 tbsp. honey
- O ¼ cup (60 ml) soy sauce
- O ¼ tsp. dried red pepper flakes
- O 1 tsp. sesame seeds
- O 2 lime wedges, to serve
- O Cooked rice (page 113), to serve

1. Heat 1 tablespoon of the oil in a large nonstick skillet over high heat. Add the onion and garlic, season with salt, and reduce the heat to medium. Sauté, stirring frequently, for 5 to 7 minutes, or until the onion is soft, taking care not to let it burn.

2. Add the broccoli to the pan and toss to combine. Sauté for 7 to 10 minutes, or until the broccoli is crisp-tender.

3. Add the mushrooms, pepper, squash, and snow peas. Sauté for an additional 5 minutes, or until the vegetables have softened but are still brightly colored.

4. Combine the remaining 2 tablespoons oil, rice vinegar, honey, soy sauce, and red pepper flakes in a small bowl. Whisk to combine.

5. Pour the soy sauce mixture over the vegetables. Simmer for 2 minutes, or until the sauce coats the vegetables and has thickened slightly. Sprinkle with the sesame seeds. Serve immediately with cooked rice and lime wedges on the side.

TIP: To up the protein factor, add leftover cooked chicken, sliced steak, or cubed tofu to the pan after the second batch of vegetables.

Stir-Fry Inspiration

Be sure to chop everything the same size so that each ingredient cooks evenly. You'll be on your way to dinner bliss in no time!

1. Heat the oil, add the aromatics, and stir-fry for 5 to 7 minutes, until softened but not browned.

AROMATICS:
- Onions, chopped
- Shallots, sliced
- Leeks, sliced
- Celery, sliced
- Garlic, minced
- Ginger, minced or grated

2. Add the hard vegetables. Stir-fry for 7 to 10 minutes, until crisp-tender.

THE HARD STUFF:
- Beans, cut into 1-inch (2.5 cm) pieces
- Carrots, cut into ¼-inch (5 mm) rounds
- Bell peppers, sliced

3. Add quick-cook veggies. Stir-fry for 2 to 3 minutes, until the veggies are crisp-tender.

QUICK COOKERS:
• Asparagus, cut into ½-inch (1.5 cm) pieces
• Summer squash or zucchini, cut into 1-inch (2.5 cm) cubes
• Spinach, shredded
• Kale, shredded
• Greens, shredded
• Mushrooms, sliced
• Pea pods or snow peas
• Bean sprouts

4. Add the sauce. You can also add flavors like 1 teaspoon grated ginger or ¼ teaspoon Sichuan pepper to the sauce, or sweeten it up by stirring in ¼ cup (35 g) mango or pineapple chunks at the end.

5. Instead of sesame seeds, finish the dish with a handful of cashews, or a couple of sliced green onions, or chopped cilantro.

Clever Quiche

SERVES : 6–8
PREPARATION TIME : 10 MINUTES
COOKING TIME : 1 HOUR

Whether it's for breakfast, lunch, or dinner, quiche is a great all-in-one dish. I made this one during a fridge clearout, but you can create your own filling combination.

SHOPPING LIST

- One 9-inch (23 cm) refrigerated piecrust
- 1 tbsp. olive oil
- ½ onion, chopped
- 1 cup (60 g) sliced white mushrooms
- 1½ packed cups (30 g) baby spinach
- 1 cup (240 ml) heavy cream
- 5 large eggs
- ½ tsp. salt
- ¼ tsp. pepper
- 6 slices bacon, cooked and crumbled
- ¼ cup (30 g) crumbled feta cheese

1. Preheat the oven to 375°F (190°C). Unroll the piecrust and arrange it in the bottom of a 9-inch (23 cm) deep-dish pie plate.

2. Heat the oil in a large skillet over medium heat. Add the onion and mushrooms and cook for 8 to 10 minutes, stirring occasionally, until soft and golden. Reduce the heat to low and add the spinach. Cook for 1 minute, or until wilted. Remove from the heat.

3. In a large bowl, whisk together the cream, eggs, salt, and pepper. Stir in veggies, bacon, and cheese. Pour the mixture into the prepared piecrust.

4. Bake 35 to 45 minutes, or until a toothpick or a strand of uncooked spaghetti inserted near the center of the filling comes out clean, and the filling doesn't jiggle. Let cool on a wire rack for 10 to 15 minutes before cutting and serving.

TIPS: Any leftovers are great for lunch the next day with a side salad. If your piecrust is frozen, defrost it in the fridge while you're at work.

Quiche Inspiration

Classic quiche filling combinations include the following:

MEAT FILLINGS
- Ham and Gruyère cheese (Quiche Lorraine)
- Ham and Swiss cheese
- Leek and bacon
- Chicken and mushroom
- Chicken and asparagus

FISH FILLINGS
- Smoked salmon, goat cheese, and dill
- Salmon and spinach
- Smoked salmon and shrimp
- Smoked mackerel and tomato

VEGETABLE FILLINGS
- Broccoli and Cheddar cheese
- Tomato, mozzarella, and basil
- Tomato, zucchini, and Parmesan
- Cheddar cheese and caramelized onions
- Goat cheese and watercress
- Zucchini, feta, and dill

Zero-Waste Options

So, that dish called for two carrots. Now what do you do with the rest of the bag?

I've brainstormed classic recipe ideas for common leftover ingredients, so all you have to do is find a recipe, and get cooking. There are some recipes in this section that are ideal—or look in the other chapters for ideas. And don't forget that many ingredients freeze well and can be used later.

Carrots

- Carrot Soup
- Carrot Cake
- Carrot Salad
- Roasted Carrots
- Glazed Carrots
- ❄ Peel and slice into medallions and freeze.

Tomatoes

- Roasted Tomato-Basil Soup (see opposite page)
- Fresh Tomato Sauce
- Roasted Tomatoes
- Tomato Salad
- Stuffed Tomatoes
- Salsa
- Gazpacho
- Bruschetta
- ❄ Do not freeze.
- 🔥 Slice the tomatoes and put on a baking tray lined with parchment paper. Let dry in the oven at 200°F (90°C) for 6 to 12 hours, or until leathery, checking often. Store the dried tomatoes in olive oil in an airtight jar. Refrigerate and use within three weeks.

Onions

- Sliced on pizza or burgers (page 50)
- French Onion Soup
- Fried Onions
- Caramelized Onion Tart
- Pickled Onions
- ❄ Slice or dice and freeze.

Lettuce

- Lettuce Soup
- Salad
- Lettuce Wraps
- Spring Rolls
- Grilled lettuce
- Noodle Bowls
- Stir-Fried lettuce
- ❄ Do not freeze.

Roasted Tomato-Basil Soup

SERVES : 2
PREPARATION TIME : 10 MINUTES
COOKING TIME : 30 MINUTES

Homemade tomato soup is so much better than the canned stuff! Plus, the avocado in this recipe makes the soup so creamy that you won't miss the dairy at all!

SHOPPING LIST

- 1¼ lb. (570 g) tomatoes, halved lengthwise
- 3 cloves garlic, peeled and smashed
- ½ small onion, quartered
- 1 tbsp. olive oil
- 1 tsp. salt
- ½ tsp. ground black pepper
- Flesh of ½ large avocado
- 1 cup (12 g) lightly packed fresh basil leaves, roughly torn
- 1½ cups (360 ml) vegetable broth
- Shredded basil, croutons, and olive oil, to serve

NOTES

....
....
....
....
....
....
....
....
....
....
....

1. Preheat the oven to 425°F (220ºC). Place the tomatoes, garlic, and onions on a baking tray, drizzle with oil, and season with the salt and pepper. Roast for 25 minutes, or until the tomatoes are soft. Remove from the oven and allow to cool slightly.

2. Place the tomatoes, onions, and garlic in a high-powered blender. Add the avocado, basil, and broth. Blend for 1 to 2 minutes, or until smooth.

3. Transfer the soup to a large pot and cook over a medium heat until it is piping hot. Serve with shredded basil, croutons, and a drizzle of olive oil.

TIP: The recipe is dairy-free, but if you do eat dairy, then serve topped with Parmesan shavings or with a grilled cheese sandwich on the side.

Cucumbers

- Cucumber Salad (see opposite page)
- Tzatziki
- Cucumber Sandwiches
- Pickles
- Smashed Sichuan Cucumbers
- Cucumber Gazpacho
- ❄ Do not freeze.

Cabbage

- Coleslaw (page 49)
- Cabbage Salad
- Stuffed Cabbage
- Sauerkraut
- Corned Beef and Cabbage
- Egg Rolls
- ❄ Do not freeze.

Potatoes

- Potato Salad
- Leek and Potato Soup
- Scalloped Potatoes
- Hash
- Hasselback Potatoes

Baked:

- Potato Skins
- Twice-Baked Potatoes

Mashed:

- Potato Cakes
- Duchess Potatoes
- Shepherd's Pie
- Thickener for creamy soup
- ❄ Do not freeze.

Bell Peppers

- Southwestern Stuffed Peppers
- Roasted Peppers
- Cheesesteak Sandwich
- Fajitas
- Soup
- ❄ Chop and freeze.

Cucumber Salad

SERVES : 2
PREPARATION TIME : 10 MINUTES

This light and aromatic side salad is the perfect accompaniment to grilled fish or chicken for a light supper. The vinaigrette is the star of the show.

SHOPPING LIST

- ½ fennel bulb, green fronds reserved
- 4 oz. (115 g) radishes
- ¼ large English cucumber
- 2 tbsp. mandarin juice
- 1 tbsp. red wine vinegar
- ½ garlic clove, minced
- ½ tsp salt
- ½ tsp ground black pepper
- 2 tbsp. extra virgin olive oil

NOTES

....
....
....
....
....
....
....
....
....
....
....
....
....
....

1. Using a sharp knife, thinly slice the white part of the fennel, the radishes, and the cucumber. Combine the vegetables in a large bowl.

2. In a small bowl, combine the mandarin juice, vinegar, garlic, salt, and pepper and whisk together while pouring in the olive oil in a slow, steady stream. Continue whisking the vinaigrette until the ingredients are thoroughly combined. Drizzle the dressing over the veggies.

3. Chop the fennel fronds and use to garnish the salad. Serve immediately or refrigerate for 30 minutes to let the flavors come together.

TIP: To save some time when you get home, slice all of the veggies and make the dressing the night before. Store the two separately, then combine before serving. You can substitute orange, lemon, lime, or grapefruit juice for the mandarin juice if you don't have any on hand.

Zucchini

- Savory Italian Zucchini Bread (see opposite page)
- Fried Zucchini
- Stuffed Baked Zucchini
- Sweet Zucchini Bread
- Zucchini Noodles
- Zucchini Muffins
- ❄ Do not freeze.

Beef

Ground:

- Italian Meat Sauce
- Meatballs
- Meatloaf
- Add to tacos, burritos, soups and chili.

Sliced:

- Thai Beef Salad
- Casseroles
- Add to stir-fries.
- ❄ Place cooled cooked beef or raw beef in a food-storage bag, remove as much air as possible, and lay flat to freeze.

Eggs

- Omelette
- Frittata
- Soufflé
- Quiche
- Scrambled Eggs
- Lemon Meringue Pie
- Pound Cake
- Hard-Boiled Eggs
- ❄ Do not freeze.

Bread

- Bread Pudding
- Panzanella
- Bruschetta
- French Bread Pizza
- Garlic Bread
- French Toast
- Croutons: Toast slices of stale bread and cut into cubes.
- Breadcrumbs: Grate stale bread on a coarse grater.
- ❄ Slice and freeze, then take out a slice or two at a time to toast.

Savory Italian Zucchini Bread

MAKES : 8–10 SLICES
PREPARATION TIME : 20 MINUTES
COOKING TIME : 50 MINUTES

You've probably had sweet zucchini bread, but have you ever tried a savory version? Serve with smear of salted butter or tomato jam for the ultimate snack.

SHOPPING LIST

- Canola oil, for greasing
- 3 cups (420 g) all-purpose flour
- 4 tsp. baking powder
- 1 tsp. salt
- ½ tsp. baking soda
- ½ tsp. garlic powder
- 1 cup (225 g) shredded zucchini
- ¾ cup (80 g) grated Parmesan cheese
- 1 tsp. finely chopped fresh rosemary (or ¼ tsp. dried)
- 1 tsp. dried parsley
- 1 tsp. dried basil
- 2 large eggs
- 1 cup (240 ml) whole milk
- ½ cup (115 g) sun-dried tomatoes in oil, drained and chopped
- 4 tbsp. unsalted butter, melted
- 1 sprig fresh rosemary

NOTES

....
....
....
....
....
....

1. Preheat the oven to 350°F (175°C). Grease a 9" x 5" (23 x 12.5 cm) loaf pan with canola oil and set aside.

2. Place the flour, baking powder, salt, baking soda, and garlic powder in a large bowl and whisk to combine. Stir in the zucchini, Parmesan, rosemary, parsley, and basil.

3. In a separate bowl, combine the eggs, milk, sun-dried tomatoes, and butter. Pour the wet ingredients into the dry ingredients and gently stir together just until combined. Don't worry if there are flecks of flour—overstirring will make the bread tough.

4. Spoon the batter into the prepared pan and place the sprig of rosemary on top. Bake for 50 minutes, or until a toothpick or uncooked strand of spaghetti inserted in the center comes out clean.

5. Cool for 10 minutes before removing from the pan and placing on a cooling rack to cool completely.

Chicken

- Sandwiches
- Chicken Salad
- Chicken Soup
- Chicken Pot Pie
- Stir-Fries
- Fried Rice
- Pasta
- Greek Chicken Salad Pitas (see opposite page)
- ❄ Shred cooled chicken, place in a food-storage bag, remove as much air as possible, and lay flat to freeze.

Cooked Rice

- Add to soups.
- Serve as a side dish.
- Fried Rice
- Cabbage Rolls
- Arancini
- Rice Bowls
- Poke Bowls
- Veggie Burgers
- Sushi
- Burritos
- ❄ Place cooled cooked rice in a food-storage bag, remove as much air as possible, and lay flat to freeze.

Cooked Pasta

- Noodle Kugel
- Soups
- Baked Pasta
- Mac 'n' Cheese (page 82)
- Frittata
- Pasta Salad
- ❄ Do not freeze.

Parsley

- Tabbouleh
- Pesto
- Gremolata
- ❄ Chop finely and freeze.

FREEZING & DRYING HERBS

Use this method to freeze parsley and other fresh herbs such as cilantro, basil, and sage.

❄ Rinse the herbs, chop finely, place 1 tablespoon of chopped herbs in each compartment of an ice-cube tray, cover with water, then freeze. Once frozen, remove the cubes from the tray and store in a plastic bag in the freezer. Add cubes of frozen herbs to stews or soups.

🔥 Herbs can be dried in the microwave. Rinse the herbs. Lay on a piece of paper towel, then place a second piece on top. Cook in the microwave on high for 2 minutes. If the leaves are not dry and brittle, heat for another 30 seconds. Crumble the herbs and place in an airtight container. They will keep in a cool, dark place for up to one year.

Greek Chicken Salad Pitas

SERVES : 2
PREPARATION TIME : 40 MINUTES

Chicken salad is great option for lunch or dinner. The best part is that you can prep a few hours ahead, store it in the fridge, and have it ready when you're hungry.

- ¼ cup (60 ml) Greek yogurt
- 2 tsp. lemon juice
- 1 garlic clove, minced
- ⅓ medium cucumber, peeled, seeded and chopped
- 2 cups (230 g) cooked diced chicken breast
- 1 large Roma tomato, chopped
- ¼ cup (30 g) crumbled feta cheese
- 10 Kalamata olives, pitted and chopped
- 2 tsp. chopped fresh parsley
- ¼ tsp. salt
- ¼ tsp. pepper
- 2 pita breads, to serve

NOTES

....
....
....
....
....
....
....
....
....
....

1. Combine all of the ingredients, except for the pitas, in a large bowl and mix well to combine. Chill for 30 minutes.

2. When you are ready to serve the pitas, cut them in half to make four pockets. Spoon salad into each half and serve immediately.

TIP: Try toasting your pitas before stuffing them with the chicken salad for an extra crunch. Or pile the salad on your favorite crackers for a filling mid-day bite.

THE BASICS

Every great main dish deserves a standout side or superior sauce. These are the go-to recipes I turn to meal after meal.

Marinara Sauce

SERVES : 8
PREPARATION TIME : 5 MINUTES
COOKING TIME : 20 MINUTES

Marinara sauce is essential to have on hand in your kitchen, whether you're craving a bowl of spaghetti and meatballs or a plate of chicken Parmesan.

SHOPPING LIST

- 2 tbsp. olive oil
- 6 garlic cloves, peeled and sliced (or minced)
- One 28-oz. (800 g) can crushed tomatoes
- ⅛ tsp. crushed red pepper flakes (or a pinch of cayenne pepper)
- 1½ tsp. salt
- ¼ tsp. ground black pepper
- ¼ tsp. dried oregano
- 1 tsp. dried basil

NOTES

....
....
....
....
....
....
....
....

1. Heat the oil in a large sauté pan over medium-high heat. Add the garlic and sauté for 1 minute, stirring frequently, until fragrant. Stir in the tomatoes, red pepper flakes, salt, pepper, oregano, and basil.

2. Continue cooking until the sauce starts to simmer. Reduce the heat to medium-low and simmer for 15 minutes, until thick and smooth.

TIP: Try doubling the ingredients and freezing portions for later. Let the sauce cool completely then spoon into freezer bags. Place the sealed bags on a baking sheet in your freezer so they freeze flat. Freeze for up to 3 months and defrost before reheating.

SERVES : 2
PREPARATION TIME : 5 MINUTES
COOKING TIME : 30 MINUTES

Easy Mashed Potatoes

SHOPPING LIST

- O 3 medium Yukon Gold potatoes, peeled and cut into quarters
- O 1 tbsp. unsalted butter
- O ½ cup (120 ml) whole milk
- O 1 oz. (30 g) cream cheese, at room temperature
- O ½ tsp. salt
- O ¼ tsp. black pepper

1. Fill a medium saucepan with water and season liberally with salt. Add potatoes and bring to a boil over high heat. Lower the heat and simmer for 20 minutes, until the potatoes fall apart when pierced with a fork.

2. Drain the potatoes and return to the same pan over medium heat. Add the butter and cook for 2 to 3 minutes, stirring with a wooden spoon to break up the potatoes.

3. Add the milk, cream cheese, and salt and pepper. Stir constantly until the potatoes are smooth, about 2 to 3 minutes. Serve immediately.

SERVES : 2
PREPARATION TIME : 5 MINUTES
COOKING TIME : 25 MINUTES

Foolproof Rice

SHOPPING LIST

- O ⅔ cup (125 g) white or brown basmati rice
- O 1 cup (240 ml) water

1. Combine the rice and water in a small saucepan with a tight-fitting lid. Bring to a boil over high heat, then turn off the heat without opening the lid. Let stand for 25 minutes without lifting the lid. Fluff the rice with a fork and serve immediately.

TIP: This rice is unseasoned so that you can use it in or with a multitude of other dishes. If you wish to have it by itself, add ¾ teaspoon of salt to the saucepan before boiling.

SERVES : 2
PREPARATION TIME : 5 MINUTES

Classic Salad Dressing

SHOPPING LIST

- O 2 tbsp. red wine vinegar
- O 2 tsp. Dijon mustard
- O ½ tsp. salt
- O ¼ tsp black pepper
- O ⅓–½ cup (80–120 ml) olive oil

1. Whisk together the vinegar, mustard, salt, and pepper. Slowly stream in the olive oil, whisking constantly, until the desired consistency is reached.

TIP: Once you have this base recipe down, you can build on it with other ingredients you have at home. Try whisking in 1 teaspoon of honey for added sweetness, or 1 tablespoon of fresh chopped herbs or 1 minced shallot for added flavor. Store any leftover dressing in a sealed jar in the fridge for up to 5 days.

PART 3

TEMPLATES

Best Ever
BREAKFASTS

RECIPE	SOURCE	☆ ☆ ☆ ☆ ☆	NOTES

RECIPE	SOURCE	☆ ☆ ☆ ☆ ☆	NOTES

RECIPE	SOURCE	☆ ☆ ☆ ☆ ☆	NOTES

RECIPE	SOURCE	☆ ☆ ☆ ☆ ☆	NOTES

RECIPE	SOURCE	☆ ☆ ☆ ☆ ☆	NOTES

RECIPE	SOURCE	☆ ☆ ☆ ☆ ☆	NOTES

RECIPE	SOURCE	☆ ☆ ☆ ☆ ☆	NOTES

RECIPE	SOURCE	☆ ☆ ☆ ☆ ☆	NOTES

RECIPE	SOURCE	☆ ☆ ☆ ☆ ☆	NOTES

RECIPE	SOURCE	☆ ☆ ☆ ☆ ☆	NOTES

Holiday FAVORITES

RECIPE	SOURCE	☆ ☆ ☆ ☆ ☆	NOTES

RECIPE	SOURCE	☆ ☆ ☆ ☆ ☆	NOTES

To share with
FRIENDS

RECIPE	SOURCE	☆ ☆ ☆ ☆ ☆	NOTES

RECIPE	SOURCE	☆ ☆ ☆ ☆ ☆	NOTES

Favorites from my COOKBOOKS

RECIPE	SOURCE	☆ ☆ ☆ ☆ ☆	NOTES

RECIPE	SOURCE	☆ ☆ ☆ ☆ ☆	NOTES

RECIPE	SOURCE	☆ ☆ ☆ ☆ ☆	NOTES

RECIPE	SOURCE	☆ ☆ ☆ ☆ ☆	NOTES

WISH LIST
COOKBOOKS

TITLE	AUTHOR	NOTES

TITLE	AUTHOR	NOTES

WISH LIST

EQUIPMENT

ITEM	COST	WHERE TO BUY

ITEM	COST	WHERE TO BUY

PANTRY ESSENTIALS

RICE, PASTA, AND GRAINS

- ○ LONG-GRAIN WHITE RICE
- ○ BROWN RICE
- ○ PASTA (E.G. SPAGHETTI, TAGLIATELLE, LINGUINE, PENNE, FUSILLI, MACARONI)
- ○ NOODLES (E.G. EGG, RICE)
- ○ COUSCOUS
- ○ QUINOA
- ○ CORNMEAL
- ○ ROLLED OATS
- ○ BREAD CRUMBS (PLAIN OR PANKO)
- ○ TORTILLAS
- ○
- ○
- ○
- ○
- ○

BAKING ESSENTIALS

- ○ ALL-PURPOSE FLOUR
- ○ WHITE SUGAR
- ○ BROWN SUGAR
- ○ BAKING POWDER
- ○ BAKING SODA
- ○ VANILLA EXTRACT
- ○ CHOCOLATE CHIPS
- ○ COCOA POWDER
- ○ CONFECTIONERS' SUGAR
- ○ BROWN SUGAR
- ○ MAPLE SYRUP
- ○ HONEY
- ○ CORNSTARCH
- ○
- ○
- ○

CANNED GOODS

- ○ TOMATOES
- ○ TUNA
- ○ BLACK BEANS
- ○ GARBANZO BEANS
- ○ CANNELLINI BEANS
- ○ CHICKEN OR VEGETABLE BROTH
- ○ OLIVES
- ○ CHILES (E.G. CHIPOTLES IN ADOBO OR PICKLED JALAPEÑOS)
- ○ SALSA
- ○ TOMATO PASTE
- ○ ROASTED BELL PEPPERS
- ○ COCONUT MILK
- ○
- ○
- ○

CHEF'S ESSENTIALS

- ○ OLIVE OIL
- ○ VEGETABLE OIL
- ○ SALT
- ○ BLACK PEPPERCORNS IN A GRINDER
- ○ SOY SAUCE
- ○ MUSTARD (E.G. FRENCH, WHOLE-GRAIN)
- ○ VINEGAR (E.G. RED WINE, WHITE WINE, APPLE CIDER, BALSAMIC, RICE)
- ○ KETCHUP
- ○ MAYONNAISE
- ○ PICKLES
- ○ WORCESTERSHIRE SAUCE
- ○ FISH SAUCE
- ○ SESAME OIL
- ○ HOT SAUCE (E.G. SRIRACHA, SWEET CHILI SAUCE)
- ○ SESAME SEEDS
- ○ FISH SAUCE
- ○ MIRIN
- ○
- ○

DRINKS

- ○ TEA
- ○ COFFEE
- ○ CHOCOLATE
- ○ JUICE
- ○
- ○
- ○

SNACKS

- ○ CRACKERS
- ○ DRIED FRUIT (E.G. RAISINS, CRANBERRIES, APRICOTS)
- ○ SEEDS (E.G. FLAX, PUMPKIN, SUNFLOWER)
- ○ PEANUT BUTTER OR ALMOND BUTTER
- ○ APPLESAUCE
- ○
- ○
- ○
- ○
- ○
- ○
- ○
- ○
- ○

FRIDGE AND FREEZER

- ○ MILK
- ○ EGGS
- ○ CHEESE (E.G. CHEDDAR, SWISS, MOZZARELLA)
- ○ BUTTER
- ○ FROZEN VEGETABLES (E.G. PEAS, CORN, GREEN BEANS)
- ○
- ○
- ○
- ○
- ○
- ○

WEEKLY SHOPPING LIST

MEALS:

Monday	
Tuesday	
Wednesday	
Thursday	
Friday	
Saturday	
Sunday	

PANTRY

LEFTOVERS TO USE

MEAT AND FISH

FRESH PRODUCE

FRIDGE

DRINKS

FREEZER

OTHER

BUDGET: **SPENT:**   **DIFFERENCE:**

BUDGET TRACKER

WEEK:

GROCERIES:

○

○

○

○

○

○

○

EATING OUT:

○

○

○

○

○

○

○

OTHER FOOD COSTS:

BUDGET:

TOTAL EXPENSES:

DIFFERENCE:

WEEK:

GROCERIES:

○

○

○

○

○

○

○

EATING OUT:

○

○

○

○

○

○

○

OTHER FOOD COSTS:

BUDGET:

TOTAL EXPENSES:

DIFFERENCE:

MONTH:

WEEK:

GROCERIES:

○

○

○

○

○

○

○

EATING OUT:

○

○

○

○

○

○

○

OTHER FOOD COSTS:

BUDGET:

TOTAL EXPENSES:

DIFFERENCE:

WEEK:

GROCERIES:

○

○

○

○

○

○

○

EATING OUT:

○

○

○

○

○

○

○

OTHER FOOD COSTS:

BUDGET:

TOTAL EXPENSES:

DIFFERENCE:

TOTAL BUDGET: **TOTAL SPENT:**   **DIFFERENCE:**

YEARLY MEAL PLANNER

	JANUARY	FEBRUARY	MARCH	APRIL	MAY	JUNE
1						
2						
3						
4						
5						
6						
7						
8						
9						
10						
11						
12						
13						
14						
15						
16						
17						
18						
19						
20						
21						
22						
23						
24						
25						
26						
27						
28						
29						
30						
31						

	JULY	AUGUST	SEPTEMBER	OCTOBER	NOVEMBER	DECEMBER
1						
2						
3						
4						
5						
6						
7						
8						
9						
10						
11						
12						
13						
14						
15						
16						
17						
18						
19						
20						
21						
22						
23						
24						
25						
26						
27						
28						
29						
30						
31						

MONTHLY MEAL PLANNER

1	2	3	4
8	9	10	11
15	16	17	18
22	23	24	25
29	30	31	

5	6	7
12	13	14
19	20	21
26	27	28

WEEKLY MEAL PLANNER

	Monday	Tuesday	Wednesday
Breakfast			
Mid-Morning Snack			
Lunch			
Afternoon Snack			
Dinner			

Thursday	Friday	Saturday	Sunday

HABIT TRACKERS

HABIT:

1	2	3	4	5	6
7	8	9	10	11	12
13	14	15	16	17	18
19	20	21	22	23	24
25	26	27	28	29	30
31					

HABIT:

1	2	3	4	5	6
7	8	9	10	11	12
13	14	15	16	17	18
19	20	21	22	23	24
25	26	27	28	29	30
31					

HABIT:

1	2	3	4	5	6
7	8	9	10	11	12
13	14	15	16	17	18
19	20	21	22	23	24
25	26	27	28	29	30
31					

HABIT:

1	2	3	4	5	6
7	8	9	10	11	12
13	14	15	16	17	18
19	20	21	22	23	24
25	26	27	28	29	30
31					

HABIT:

1	2	3	4	5	6
7	8	9	10	11	12
13	14	15	16	17	18
19	20	21	22	23	24
25	26	27	28	29	30
31					

HABIT:

1	2	3	4	5	6
7	8	9	10	11	12
13	14	15	16	17	18
19	20	21	22	23	24
25	26	27	28	29	30
31					

HABIT:

1	2	3	4	5	6
7	8	9	10	11	12
13	14	15	16	17	18
19	20	21	22	23	24
25	26	27	28	29	30
31					

HABIT:

1	2	3	4	5	6
7	8	9	10	11	12
13	14	15	16	17	18
19	20	21	22	23	24
25	26	27	28	29	30
31					

DINNER PARTY PLANNER

DATE AND TIME:

MENU

STARTER
- ○
- ○
- ○
- ○
- ○

MAIN COURSE
- ○
- ○
- ○
- ○
- ○
- ○

DESSERT
- ○
- ○
- ○
- ○
- ○

DRINKS
- ○
- ○
- ○

PARTY ESSENTIALS

GUEST LIST
- ○
- ○
- ○
- ○
- ○

SPECIAL DIETS
- ○
- ○
- ○

MUSIC
- ○
- ○
- ○
- ○

DON'T FORGET
- ○
- ○
- ○
- ○
- ○
- ○

SHOPPING LIST

STARTER
- ○
- ○
- ○
- ○
- ○

MAIN COURSE
- ○
- ○
- ○
- ○
- ○
- ○

DESSERT
- ○
- ○
- ○
- ○

DRINKS
- ○
- ○
- ○

DECORATIONS
- ○
- ○
- ○

EQUIPMENT
- ○
- ○
- ○

TIMETABLE

THE DAY BEFORE
- ○
- ○
- ○
- ○
- ○
- ○

ON THE DAY

MORNING:
- ○
- ○
- ○
- ○
- ○
- ○

AFTERNOON & EVENING:
- ○ 12:00 PM
- ○ 1:00 PM
- ○ 2:00 PM
- ○ 3:00 PM
- ○ 4:00 PM
- ○ 5:00 PM
- ○ 6:00 PM
- ○ 6:30 PM
- ○ 6:45 PM
- ○ 7:00 PM
- ○ 7:30 PM
- ○ 8:00 PM
- ○ 8:30 PM
- ○ 9:00 PM

Index

Use the index in this book to keep track of your favorite dishes in other books, magazines, and websites. We have left space under each letter for you to add your own entries so you know where to find the recipes for other meals you love.

Acknowledgments

Without the readers of my blog, My Modern Cookery, opportunities such as this book wouldn't be presented to me. I'm humbled that you discovered my portion of the internet, took a liking to my recipes, and stuck around to see me grow.

Thank you to Sterling Publishing and Toucan Books for taking a chance on a first-time author with a lot of ideas. Without the long hours of Ellen Dupont, Julie Brooke, Leah Germann, and Elysia Liang, this book would just be a jumble of recipes and long-winded notes from a food blogger.

To Matt, my best friend, husband, and the driving force behind my success. Without you, this book wouldn't have been the least bit possible. Whether I need help with photos, taste-testing, or emotional support, he's always there to lend a helping hand without asking for anything in return.

Thank you to my parents, Chris and Renee Rhodes, for being my constant cheerleaders and making me believe that I'm capable of achieving my dreams.

Finally, for my number one motivation, my daughter, Norah. Even though she wasn't born until after the book was finished, she kept me company through every long night and early morning. Thank you, baby girl, for giving me all the motivation I needed to accomplish this milestone. I hope I make you proud.

Picture Credits